CHINA: LAND OF FAMINE

MALLORY

FIG. 1. A FARMER OF NORTHERN CHINA

"There is no other peasantry in the world which gives such an impression of absolute genuineness and of belonging so much to the soil. Here the whole of life and the whole of death takes place on the inherited ground. Man belongs to the soil, not the soil to man; it will never let its children go. However much they may increase in number, they remain upon it, wringing from Nature her scanty gifts by ever more assiduous labour."

KEYSERLING: *The Travel Diary of a Philosopher.*

AMERICAN GEOGRAPHICAL SOCIETY

SPECIAL PUBLICATION NO. 6

Edited by G. M. WRIGLEY

CHINA: LAND OF FAMINE

BY

WALTER H. MALLORY

Secretary, China International Famine Relief Commission

WITH A FOREWORD BY

DR. JOHN H. FINLEY

President of the American Geographical Society

AMERICAN GEOGRAPHICAL SOCIETY

BROADWAY AT 156TH STREET

NEW YORK

1926

COMMONWEALTH PRESS, WORCESTER, MASS.

TO MY WIFE

ALICE EVANS MALLORY

WHOSE INSPIRATION AND ENCOURAGEMENT

HAVE DONE MUCH TO MAKE POSSIBLE THIS WORK

IT IS AFFECTIONATELY

INSCRIBED

CONTENTS

FOREWORD

There could be no better preface to this authoritative and interesting work on the Land of Famine than the pictures of country life in the interior of China from Count Keyserling's "Travel Diary of a Philosopher," suggesting in one paragraph first how famine is being constantly fought by the yellow men in their blue jerkins, making the very hills which they cultivate to their summits fortresses of defense, and then how famine saps its way in through the ancestral graves and takes the living as prisoners by reason of their devotion to their dead and of their unwillingness to leave them in order to seek their livelihood and, so, fight famine in distant fields.

Every inch of soil is in cultivation, carefully manured, well and professionally tilled, right up to the highest tops of the hills, which, like the pyramids of Egypt, slope down in artificial terraces. The villages, built of clay and surrounded by clay walls, have the effect of natural forms in this landscape: they hardly stand out against the brown background. And wherever I cast my eyes, I see the peasants at work, methodically, thoughtfully, contentedly. It is they who everywhere give life to the wide plain. The blue of their jerkins is as much a part of the picture as the green of the tilled fields and the bright yellow of the dried-up river-beds. One cannot even imagine this flat land devoid of the enlivening presence of these yellow human beings. And it represents at the same time one great cemetery of immeasurable vastness. There is hardly a plot of ground which does not carry numerous grave mounds; again and again the plough must piously wend its way between the tombstones. There is no other peasantry in the world which gives such an impression of absolute genuineness and of belonging so much to the soil. Here the whole of life and the whole of death takes place on the inherited ground. Man belongs to the soil, not the soil to man; it will never let its children go. However much they may increase in number, they remain upon it, wringing from Nature her scanty gifts by ever more assiduous labour; and when they are dead, they return in child-like confidence to what is to them the real womb of their mother. And there they continue to live for evermore. The Chinese peasant, like the prehistoric Greek, believes in the life of what seems dead to us. The soil exhales the spirit of his ancestors, it is they who repay his labour and who punish him for his omissions. Thus, the inherited fields are at the same time his history, his memory, his reminiscences; he can deny it as little as he can deny himself; for he is only a part of it.

"The plough among the tombstones" is the summarizing phrase describing China's agriculture and ancestral worship— "the universal religion of the country." Mr. Mallory, in speaking of the social causes of famine, says that the most thickly populated regions where the land is good and where it is most needed for agriculture are "just the districts where graves are most numerous." This is the physical side of it, but deeper than that is the filial devotion which like a centripetal spiritual force holds the descendants to the tombs of those who have gone before. There are natural causes, economic causes, and political causes which Mr. Mallory presents, clearly and convincingly, but down at bottom is this profound social cause which he recognizes and which must be reckoned with in dealing with the things that are seen.

As Keyserling suggests, the Chinese peasant and the early Greek have something in common, as this prayer of an ancient farmer preserved to us out of that time witnesses—the prayer of one who was held to his ancestral plot, inadequate though it was.

To Demeter of the winnowing fan and the Seasons whose feet are in the furrows, Heronax lays here from a poor little plough-land their share of ears from the threshing floor, and these mixed seeds of pulse on a slabbed table the least of a little; for no great inheritance is this he has gotten him here on barren hill.

The problem in China is due primarily to the fact that the "no great inheritance" grows less and less for the individual with the multiplying of the heritors; and the multiplying force is the necessity, felt by the worshipper of the past, of "providing sufficient male children so that, in spite of the ravages of disease, accident, wars, pestilence or famine [to which the multiplying contributes] at least one will survive to carry on the family name and perform the necessary duties required by ancestor worship." The Manchurian wheat fields make vain permanent appeal to those who feel this filial and paternal obligation, even though they may go in numbers to help with a season's harvest. There is a pioneer belt along the northern front of China in Manchuria and Mongolia which could accommodate millions upon millions of ill-fed or starving Chinese farther south. If such fields were open to settlement and cultivation in America, there would be such a rush as there was a few years ago to the last frontier lands in Oklahoma. The American settlers would not be burdened in their flight by their Lares and Penates, as was Aeneas of old, who not only bore them with him but carried his father on his shoulder. The Chinese peasant says, however, in the face of like allurement: "Who would take care of the graves of my ancestors?"

Our own civilization, one of whose Ten Commandments enjoins parental reverence, but one of whose chief concerns now is the want of respect by youth for age, and by the present for the past, must find something to praise in a people who are willing to make sacrifices even to the point of starvation in order to honor not only their parents but their remote forbears. Our scientists are beginning to be concerned about spaces for libraries and cemeteries, but it is an economic anxiety. It ought not to be necessary to destroy this sense of spiritual continuity in order to fight famine in China, but it must be taken into account in all the plans for controlling floods, fighting pestilence, increasing soil fertility, improving methods of cultivation for the fields and conservation for the forests, using modern agricultural implements, making fuller use of time, avoiding waste effort, developing means of transportation and providing for credits. All these things seem to wait upon a better political organization and control, but, as Mr. Mallory urges, amelioration may be achieved even without a unified empire.

It is a shocking fact that with all the labor expended and virtues practiced, nearly a fourth of the people of the globe live in a land of famine—not of general famine at any one time nor of continuous famine in any one place, but of famine in one or another province or locality all the time. "There was a famine in the land" was a frequent phrase in ancient history.

It is somewhat discreditable to present world agriculture with its surplusage in some regions that other regions should be chronically in that condition. Mr. Mallory makes constructive suggestions, which need not be anticipated here, but it is well to give the reader who pauses to read this prefatory note the advice that one who enters the rather dark passages reciting the causes of famine in China need not abandon hope for China—for at the end one comes out into the light of day again with this assurance from the guide:

If history teaches us anything, she teaches that a race as numerous and as fundamentally sound as the Chinese, which has maintained its political and cultural solidarity for so many centuries, will not perish from the earth.

The American Geographical Society, which is interested in the whole earth, makes this sympathetic scientific contribution to the desired welfare of our antipodes, who are rich in natural resources and have almost unlimited human energy.

JOHN H. FINLEY

PREFACE

The meager knowledge in Western countries of things Chinese makes it incumbent upon those who have had the privilege of intimate association with China's problems to record their knowledge, or even their impressions, in some permanent form. The writer presents this book to discharge his obligation in this connection. It is, so far as he knows, the first to be published in English dealing exclusively with one of China's major problems, namely, famine.

It has been the writer's purpose to set forth in these pages, as briefly and understandably as possible, why China has so many famines and what, in his judgment, can be done to prevent them. No effort has been made to give a history of past disasters, excepting for purposes of illustration, and the good and bad practices of former times are alluded to only in order to throw light on conditions as they are today.

Some repetition will be discerned. This was unavoidable, for many factors are associated in the causes of famine; and its cure can come only through correlated improvements of a widely divergent nature. While treating these causes and cures individually, therefore, the writer may have traversed ground previously trodden, but only for the purpose of focusing attention on the relation of cause with cause, and cure with cure.

The author wishes gratefully to acknowledge the assistance he has received from Mr. J. E. Baker, Advisor to the Chinese Government, Mr. Y. S. Djang, Chief Secretary, Chinese Red Cross Society, Professor J. B. Tayler of Yenching University, and Mr. O. J. Todd, Chief Engineer, China International Famine Relief Commission, for criticisms and helpful suggestions in portions of the book where their expert knowledge of the particular points involved made their advice appropriate. He wishes especially to record his appreciation of the help of Mr. Carl W. Bishop, of the Smithsonian Institution, and of Mr. H. B. Elliston, of the Chinese Government Bureau of Economic Information, whose intimate knowledge, the one on the cultural and the other on the economic side of Chinese life, has made their aid of inestimable value.

Acknowledgment must also be made to the China International Famine Relief Commission for the photographic illustrations selected from its file and adding so much to the value of this volume. All those which are not otherwise credited were taken by Mr. O. J. Todd.

W. H. M.

Peking, China, April 6, 1926.

FIG. 2—A Chinese village turning out *en masse* to see the foreign visitors.

INTRODUCTION

Food is the most urgent problem of the Chinese. This fact is reflected even in the speech of the people. In China the polite salutation on meeting a friend is "Have you eaten?" instead of the customary inquiry as to one's health or well-being usually employed in other tongues. This form of greeting is a creation of the rural community, and the implication is that if the person so saluted has not eaten the inquirer will see that his needs are quickly met. Foreigners who study the language with a Chinese teacher find that almost the first words and phrases given to them have to do with food, eating, and money (with which to buy food). "The rich man has food to eat, the poor man has none," forms the basis of one of the first lessons. Beggars are referred to in the colloquial idiom as "food wanters"; and they all provide themselves with pails or bowls in which they can receive the refuse from the tables of the well-to-do.

The food problem is an ancient one in China: from the earliest times famines have been an ever recurring scourge. A study recently completed by the Student Agricultural Society of the University of Nanking brought to light the surprising and significant fact that between the years 108 B. C. and 1911 A.D. there were 1828 famines, or one nearly every year in some one of the provinces. Untold millions have died of starvation. In fact the normal death rate may be said to contain a constant famine factor. Depleted vitality following years of want also tends to increase the death rate. Chinese history is filled with the details of past disasters and not only recounts at great length the nature of the calamity and its causes but names the officials under whom relief work was administered and describes the methods pursued in bringing succor to the unfortunate victims.

The Emperor Yü, who lived four thousand years ago, achieved great renown and is still regarded by the Chinese people as a national sage, for the wisdom displayed in his flood prevention work on the Yellow River. Since his time officials have repeatedly endeavored to follow his example, and fame has been more readily achieved by devising methods to relieve and prevent famine emergencies than in almost any other way.

The great drought that occurred in North China in 1920–1921, during which, according to the best obtainable information, 500,000 of the natives perished, is still fresh in the minds of the public. Mr. Dwight W. Edwards, in his comprehensive report,[1] estimates that at the height of the distress nearly 20,000,000 people were destitute. In some of the worst affected districts not only was the entire reserve of food consumed but also all other vegetation. A house-to-house canvas revealed the following bill of fare: k'ang, mixed with wheat blades, flour made of ground leaves, fuller's earth, flower seed, poplar buds, corncobs, hung ching tsai (steamed balls of some wild herb), sawdust, thistles, leaf dust, poisonous tree bean, kaoliang husks, cotton seed, elm bark, bean cakes (very unpalatable), peanut hulls, sweet potato vines ground (considered a great delicacy), roots, stone ground up into flour to piece out the ground leaves. Some of the food was so unpalatable that the children starved, refusing to eat it.

Everything of any intrinsic value was sold by the poorer people, even including the roof timbers; and interest rates rose until even 100 per cent was considered not unreasonable in some places. There was extensive migration of the people from the dry regions, in some localities whole villages moving out. The sale of women and children, particularly young girls, reached such proportions that a special committee was organized for the protection of children. Prices ranged

[1] The North China Famine 1920–1921, With Special Reference to the West Chihli Area: Being the Report of the Peking United International Famine Relief Committee, Peking, 1922.

from $3.00 to $150.00, Chinese currency (one dollar in United States currency equals approximately two Chinese dollars), and thus the sacrifice of one or two of the younger members of the family served to provide the wherewithal to purchase food for the rest. Parents were not ready to give up their children but did so rather than see them starve.

Mr. Edwards estimates that more than $37,000,000, Chinese currency, was made available to meet the needs of the sufferers. Of this more than half was administered under international auspices; and this included large sums from abroad, particularly America. At the height of their operations the international committees alone were feeding more than 7,700,000 individuals.

A notable work was accomplished. But what of the future? Has a starving population today been saved simply to die during the next famine a few years hence unless further aid is forthcoming? Is there no means by which these great disasters can be prevented?

Well wishers of China who have studied her famine problem have brought forward many schemes for improving conditions. They reflect the particular interest with which their authors are identified, ranging all the way from the fundamentalist missionary's faith that if the Chinese masses will become Christians "the Lord will provide" to the machinery salesman's idea that China's only hope is the early adoption of industrialism.

Conservancy engineers tell us that the most urgent need is the control of China's rivers to prevent devastating floods, the carrying-out of irrigation, land-reclamation, and similar projects to increase the cultivable land. Economists propose the introduction of better banking methods which will lower the interest rates and make possible the application of the surplus capital in the cities to the rural sections of the country. Or, again, they advance the proposal to relieve the pressure of population in the thickly settled regions by colonization of the vast areas of Manchuria and Mongolia. Provision of better transportation facilities is also urged so that the abundant crops of a prosperous district may be quickly and cheaply moved to a section where flood or drought may have created a condition of want.

The educator advocates the teaching of agriculture in the schools and colleges and the advanced training of foresters. He traces China's ills, particularly of the northern provinces of the country, to deforestation—a process which has been under way for centuries.

Many of those who give their thought to the social aspects of the situation point to the phenomenally high birth rate and insist, quite justly in the author's opinion, that no permanent solution of the problem of famines in China is possible until the people are content to regulate the size of their families according to their resources.

All agree that the present unusually bad conditions are in a measure traceable to the political disorganization of the country. However, there is no more appropriate time than the present to consider by what means better conditions can be brought about; and indeed there are many remedial measures that can be initiated even in these disordered days.

The question is one of such magnitude that, if any appreciable progress is to be made, all of the plans mentioned above must be followed. But there are certain types of work that will yield results more quickly than others, and it is the author's purpose not only to present plans but to examine them in some detail and endeavor to point out the relative importance of each.

FIG. 3—In famine years locusts are caught to supplement the food supply.

CHAPTER I

ECONOMIC CAUSES OF FAMINE

The struggle for existence in China is indescribably hard. The meager statistics available show a condition among the great mass of the people which westerners are at first inclined to doubt and which, when proved to their satisfaction to be true, they are never able to understand. One often hears statements about the "margin of livelihood" in China, but facts show that there is no margin at all if the population be regarded as a whole. The bare food requirements for a normal year are greater than the present production and importation of edibles, and this leads to the under-nourishment of a part of the people and the eating of unwholesome food substitutes by the poorer classes.

LACK OF STATISTICS

The lack of reliable statistics regarding conditions in rural China has made the study of famines and the adoption of methods of relief and prevention a difficult matter. Without any standards of comparison it is even difficult to determine what constitutes a state of famine. Apart from these purely statistical difficulties, foreign investigators, even those long resident in China and conversant with the language, often bring back conflicting reports from the same district. A man of a sympathetic and impressionable nature will pronounce the whole countryside in the grip of the most abject want, while the inquirer with the more practical viewpoint reports normal conditions.

5

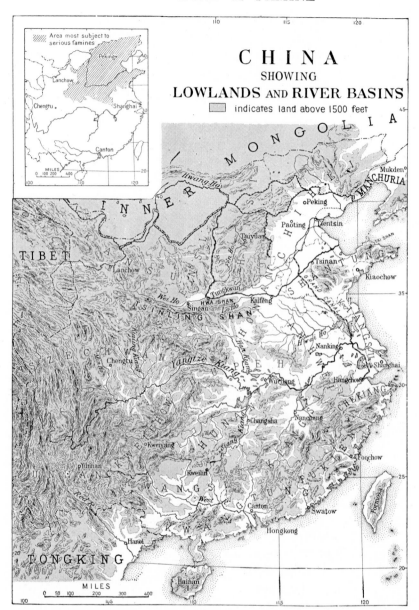

Fig. 4—Map of China showing lowlands and river basins. Scale approximately 1:23,000,000. Inset: The provinces of China most subject to serious famines, Chihli, Shantung, Shansi, Shensi, and Honan. Compare with Figure 10 showing the density of population.

Recognizing the need for more detailed and accurate information the China International Famine Relief Commission in the summer of 1922 made a survey of rural conditions. It was carried out by students from nine universities who spent their summer vacation in the country collecting data on the basis of carefully prepared questionnaires and under the supervision of professors of economics of known standing. This was probably the first scientific attempt of any importance to secure dependable facts concerning the social and economic conditions under which the country people live; and some of the results of this inquiry will be utilized in these pages.[2]

THE COST OF LIVING

Various estimates have been made of the cost of living in interior China. On account of poor transportation this cost is greatly affected by the size of the last harvest in the particular district examined; and, since these estimates always refer to restricted areas, allowance must be made if the figures are to be applied to the country as a whole.

Professor C. G. Dittmer after a detailed examination of the budgets of about 200 families near Peking reaches the conclusion that a family of five can live in comparative comfort, according to local standards, on an income of $100 a year, Chinese currency.[3] This would provide sufficient simple food, a house that would at least afford shelter from the elements, two suits of clothing for each person, enough fuel for cooking, and a surplus of $5.00 for miscellaneous expenses. However, he goes on to say that the Chinese families examined by him all lived within their incomes, even though they received no more than $50.00 a year, and that those earning $70.00 a year were able to save money. The Manchu families included in the survey all showed a deficit if their income was less than $90.00.

[2] C. B. Malone and J. B. Tayler: The Study of Chinese Rural Economy, *China Internatl. Famine Relief Comm. Publ.*, Ser. B, No. 10, Peking, 1924.

[3] C. G. Dittmer: An Estimate of the Chinese Standard of Living in China, *Quart. Journ. of Economics*, Vol. 33, 1918, pp. 107–128.

FIG. 5—Yennanfu, a city of Shensi, one of the provinces most subject to serious drought.   Note the barren eroded hills.

In Professor Dittmer's analysis of family expenses, the cost of food ranged from 68 to 83 per cent, the regular diet being two meals a day of corn bread and salt turnips. Rent averaged 5 to 15 per cent, the best house costing but $15.00 a year. Fuel and light required on the average 6 to 7 per cent of the yearly expenditure, and clothing 3.4 to 8.5 per cent. Miscellaneous expenditures (including books, recreation, savings, etc.) ranged from 1.3 to 6.6 per cent, and for the families with the largest incomes the average annual amount was only $8.90. This last item is a real measure of the family's standard of living. In the United States even the poorer classes have at least 20 per cent of their income remaining after the bare necessities of life are assured— more than three times the proportion enjoyed by the most fortunate Chinese families included in this survey.

The figures arrived at by Professor J. B. Tayler are somewhat higher: he gives the total annual income requirement for a family of five roughly as $150.00.[4] The higher estimate may be due in part to the fact that the investigation on which he bases his opinion was made several years after that of Professor Dittmer, and living costs had risen considerably in the meantime. It should be pointed out that his estimates are based on the requirements for the adequate sustenance of a poor family rather than on an average of what is actually spent by them. The figures obtained from rural investigation have shown that a large proportion of the incomes are below the poverty line; and to give the actual expenditure on which a family is known to have survived does not necessarily mean that its members have received sufficient food or clothing to keep them in health.

Professor Tayler's appraisal of the food requirements is founded on a model diet for a poor Chinese farming population prepared by Dr. G. Douglas Gray of the British Legation, Peking, and Professor Bernard E. Read of the Peking Union Medical College. According to this diet 104 ounces of grain (32 oz. wheat, 24 oz. millet, and 48 oz. kaoliang), 15 ounces of vegetables, 10 ounces of oil, and in winter 16 ounces of

[4] *China Internatl. Famine Relief Comm. Publ.*, Ser. B, No. 10.

cabbage are needed daily for a family of five.   This diet is
for a northern family since no rice is included.   It contains
no luxuries: there is no meat nor fish nor eggs.   It is only
about one-third of the value of the diet required in England
to yield an equal protein content and an equal number of
calories, the English diet containing a large proportion of
animal products.   Professor Tayler puts the clothing requirement at $20.00 a year, housing at $5.00, light at $5.00,
and allows $7.00 for miscellaneous expenses.   The $113.00
left from the budget of $150.00 is not enough to purchase
the food requisite for the diet given above but, allowing
for the period of inaction during the winter when the people
are able to reduce their food allowance, is sufficient to maintain life.   The cost of living in eastern and southern China is
higher than in the north, because rice is more expensive
than the northern grains; but the greater clothing and fuel
needs in the north tend to reduce the difference.

Taking the more liberal allowance of $150.00 estimated
by Professor Tayler as the poverty line, let us examine the
China International Famine Relief Commission's survey,
which covered 240 villages in Chihli, Kiangsu, Shantung,
Anhwei, and Chekiang, with a total of 7097 families, or
37,191 individuals.   We find that more than half the population of the eastern villages and more than four-fifths of
that of the northern villages had an income below the poverty
line.   No less than 17.6 per cent of the families of the eastern
villages and 62.2 per cent of those of the northern villages
had incomes of less than $50.00.   This represents not only
the actual cash income but also the value of crops raised and
earnings from village industry.   Professor Tayler says:

> The pressure of population is evidently a grim reality, and a con-
> siderable percentage of the families seem to go to pieces under this pressure.
> In the case of Chihli the figures are almost unbelievable.   It is not con-
> tended that they are exact.   In a certain number of cases the income
> given may have been very far from the truth, in many cases it may have
> been appreciably below, perhaps as much as twenty or even thirty per
> cent; but when allowance has been made for the utmost that can be
> conceded in this direction, the results still have a comparative value and
> they are certainly sufficiently startling.

It is interesting to note, for the sake of comparison, that the Peking police estimate of the income necessary for independence, as given in "Peking: A Social Survey" is $66.00 a year for a family of two and $93.00 a year for a

FIG. 6   FIG. 7

FIG. 6—The struggle for existence in China is indescribably hard. Victims of a famine.

FIG. 7—Not a famine victim, but a professional beggar.

family of four.[5] This would nearly coincide with Professor Dittmer's calculation.

Somewhat similar surveys have been made recently (1925) by the Chinese Government Bureau of Economic Information, and the results arrived at are not sufficiently different to alter these conclusions. For instance, an investigation of the current wages in Shansi, one of the most

[5] S. D. Gamble and J. S. Burgess: Peking: A Social Survey, New York, 1921, p. 268.

prosperous and well governed provinces today, shows that the rate varies from $2.00 to $7.00 a month, including board, according to the line of work. The average for all trades is $4.50 a month, or $54.00 a year, Chinese currency. Farm hands are generally engaged by the year, their remuneration with board and lodging being $15.00 to $20.00 annually. The Bureau states that wages have increased from 100 to 200 per cent during the past decade.[6]

Another investigation, the results of which were published by the same Bureau,[7] was conducted by Dr. Ta Chen, professor of sociology of Tsing Hua College, Peking. An examination was made of two villages, Chenfu, which is six miles from Peking and which may be considered as representing conditions in the north, and Huichow, Anhwei, in the rice-growing belt of central China. The following estimate of the cost of living was arrived at:

	Chenfu	Huichow
Food	$84.00	$106.60
Clothing	40.00	40.00
Rent	6.00	5.50
Miscellaneous (fuel, light)	5.00	5.00
Total expenses	$135.00	$157.10
Occupational earnings	93.12	88.80
Deficit	$41.88	$68.30

It will be seen that the cost of living is greater in the south, a result which bears out the Famine Commission figures. Also it appears that the people in neither village had sufficient income to meet the requirements of this standard of living, many of them being entirely dependent on occupational earnings. The average size of the families was 4.9 in Chenfu, and 4.4 in Huichow. These figures are slightly smaller than the findings of the Famine Commission, but they cover only 147 families, while the latter survey included 7097.

[6] *Chinese Econ. Monthly*, Vol. 2, No. 9, Chinese Govt. Bur. of Econ. Information, Peking.

[7] *Ibid.*, Vol. 2, No. 5.

Food Requirements Not Met

As has been said above, normal annual food requirements are greater than the entire domestic production plus the imports. In accordance with the diet which has been accepted as necessary to preserve health, the grain needed for a family of five is 2372 pounds a year. Mr. D. K. Lieu of the Chinese Government Bureau of Economic Information estimates that the average yield of wheat, the staple food in the northern provinces, is about 1200 pounds an acre which, after deducting loss in husking and milling, would leave 500 pounds of flour.[8] It would, therefore, take 4.7 acres to provide for a family of five. But 33 per cent of the holdings are less than one acre, and 55 per cent are one and one-half acres or less, while the number of large farms is very small indeed. The average size of the families who have as much as one and one-half acres is 5.7, and the number in the families increases with the size of the holdings. The same land in good years is capable of producing, besides the winter wheat, a crop of beans or millet which is harvested in the fall; but even assuming two crops a year which, because of frequent floods and droughts, is possible only a part of the time, it will be seen that the yield does not meet the needs.

The staple food in central and southern China is rice. Probably two-thirds of the entire population of China make it their chief diet. Mr. Lieu estimates the average yield of clean rice at 2150 pounds an acre in the richest rice-growing region. The average yield for all rice-growing provinces is probably about 1400 pounds an acre. At this rate it would take 1.7 acres to provide the 2372 pounds necessary for an average family. But, as has been said, 55 per cent of the families have holdings of less than an acre and a half. During the last three years for which statistics of the Maritime Customs are available the excess of imports of rice over exports averages about 17,000,000 piculs, or 2,260,000,000 pounds, a year. If we place the number of rice eaters at 300,000,000, this quantity divided among them would mean

[8] D. K. Lieu: Food Conservation in China, *Mid-Pacific Mag.*, Honolulu. Vol. 29, 1925, pp. 511–519.

7.5 pounds apiece. In addition, much of the land is capable of producing two crops, which helps to bring the yield up to requirements. The picture, however, is blacker when it is borne in mind that, although there is an embargo on the export of rice and of some other cereals, much smuggling is practiced and the embargo is often raised by the military dictators in times of provincial warfare in return for large contributions from interested merchants to the war chests. Chinese rice is always in demand and brings a good price in Japan; and no doubt much rice finds its way thither without being recorded by the Customs authorities.

FIG. 8—Terraced fields in the hills of Szechwan.

It will be recognized that these figures are quite general in nature and most unsatisfactory to the exact. As was remarked at the beginning of this chapter adequate statistics are lacking. One must talk in terms of specific localities, and here the figures are eloquent enough. Personal experience would corroborate the truth of the observations derived herefrom over a much wider area and in much more touching terms of human misery.

It is this lack of any margin of livelihood that is one of the fundamental causes of famine. It will be readily seen that the destruction or failure of even one crop results in severe distress and, in many cases, in actual famine. Analogous conditions in western countries result only in a period of hard times, for the population has an economic reserve on which to call.

OVERCROWDING

The density of population in China as a whole is only about 238 to the square mile.[9] This figure, however, does not show the conditions of the great mass of the people. Half of the total population of China occupies but a quarter of the total area of the coun-try. The Famine Commission investigations covering 65 vil-lages in the rice-growing provinces of Chekiang and Kiangsu have shown that the number of inhabitants to the square mile varies from 980 in some village districts to 6880 in others. In Shantung fig-ures range from 1800 to 3000, and in the northern wheat-producing province of Chihli from 550 to 2010. In the most densely peopled area in India, in parts of Bengal, there are 1162 people to the square mile of cultivated land, while in Oudh there are 816, in Agra 761, and in Madras only 615. Figures for Japan include also the cities; and the total given for the most densely peopled area is 2349 to the square mile. Japan does not produce sufficient food to support its people.

FIG. 9—One sees an occasional wood lot in southern Shensi.

It is not difficult to prove that the population saturation point has been reached on the coastal plains of China. In the early part of the nineteenth century Malthus developed his famous theory of population—that there is a tendency for the human race constantly to increase and to press upon subsistence. Subsistence, he said, only increases in arith-metical ratio, while population bounds forward in geometrical

[9] The question of Chinese population estimates is discussed in Chapter IV.

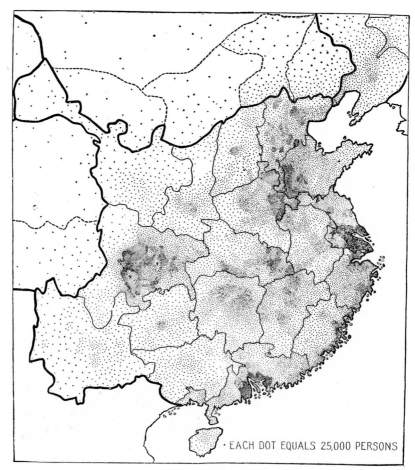

· EACH DOT EQUALS 25,000 PERSONS

FIG. 10—The density of population in China. Scale approximately 1 :27,000,000. This and the succeeding maps, Figures 11–14 showing some typical distributions by provinces, are reproduced by permission from the China Continuation Committee's survey, "The Christian Occupation of China," Shanghai, 1922.

ratio. But he also pointed out that the unequal race was counteracted in either one of two ways, which he called positive and preventive checks. The positive checks work to increase the death rate; the preventive checks to decrease the birth rate.

Before the time of Malthus, Süssmilch, the first writer on vital statistics, as early as 1750 named as the four great natural checks to the increase of mankind: pestilence "which often carried off half the population, not only of cities but of whole provinces"; war, "a real monster, a disgraceful blot on reason and humanity, and especially on Christianity"; famine; earthquakes and floods.

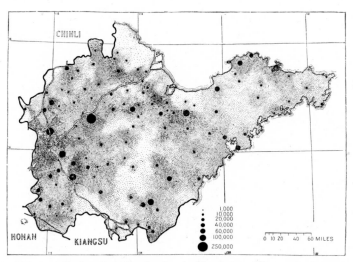

Fig. 11—Population distribution in Shantung. The western province, forming part of the great northern plain, is one of the very densely peopled regions of China. Scale approximately 1:7,500,000.

In China the birth rate is abnormally high as is also the death rate, facts which bear out Malthus' theory that the population is pressing on subsistence and reducing the standard of life. The positive check is operating, for the population tends to increase faster than the means of support justify and is held in check only by famines, disease, and war. The inhabitants are ill fed, insufficiently clothed, and ofttimes without proper shelter.

This overcrowding on the land makes impossible the collection of any reserve of foodstuffs. A good crop does not result in a surplus of grain but merely provides the people for a short time with a better diet, since the farmer is able to eat and in fact, on the average, should eat more than he can normally produce. Thus when a poor year occurs the whole countryside finds itself without food and ofttimes without the wherewithal to procure it from outside sources.

SURPLUS LABOR

There are several reasons for this overcrowding on the land, the most important being traceable to the traditional Chinese family system, which tends to hold the various branches together no matter how greatly it increases in numbers. The sons are expected to live at home with their parents and grandparents, if there are any, and when they marry their wives become full-fledged members of the family group. What little land there is must support the ever increasing numbers until a point is reached where no more can possibly subsist on the produce. Frequent famines tend to readjust this condition, and there is the beginning of a movement of the young men to urban centers where they obtain employment as servants, porters, carriers, or factory hands. Industrialization of the country, however, has not progressed so far as to effect any appreciable change in the situation except perhaps in restricted areas near the ports. The places of those who leave are soon filled, and those who go regard themselves as only temporarily absent and do not completely break away

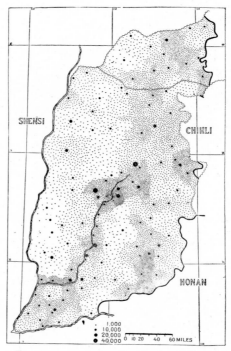

FIG. 12—Population distribution in Shansi, a province of the loess plateau. The greatest density is in the basins, especially in the Fen Ho valley.

from home. In case of a loss of employment, they drift back to increase the burden on the land.

There is a tremendous labor surplus. With only an acre and a half to an average family of 5.7 members hundreds of labor days per family are wasted in the course of a year. Village industries tend to help matters somewhat; but poor transportation, lack of capital, and lack of initiative have prevented their development to any substantial extent.

There is an annual movement of labor from Shantung which reflects to a marked degree the love of home and unwillingness to leave it for new fields. Every year more than thirty thousand men migrate from Shantung to Manchuria. They leave early in the spring and travel

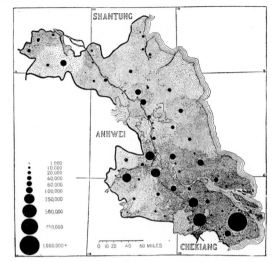

FIG. 13

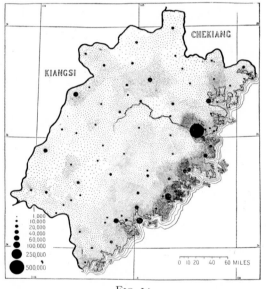

FIG. 14

FIG. 13—Population distribution in Kiangsu. The southern third of the province, part of the Yangtze delta, has an extremely high population density.

FIG. 14—Population distribution in Fukien. The population of southern China is concentrated especially on the coasts.

more than 500 miles to the rich lands of the north where
they work during the summer; but in the autumn they all return to their homes in Shantung. In the days before the construction of the Peking-Mukden Railway, they made this
trip on foot taking nearly a month on the road each way.
It is almost unbelievable that such a practice continues
year after year when good Manchurian farm lands are
available and can be bought on easy terms and for a phenomenally low price from the railway authorities which are
making an effort to settle this region. It cannot be said
that the people do not realize the benefits, for they see them
with their own eyes and share in them for a short time every
summer; but they are unwilling to change their homes and
their mode of life.

It may be said that there has been a great migration of
Chinese in the past, and this subject will be discussed in future
chapters; but the point made here is that for the most part
the movement of population at present is rather the emigration of surplus labor than any large transplantation of
family groups to new localities.

The facility with which large armies can be recruited by
the various military leaders without greatly affecting the
districts from which they are taken is a striking evidence
of the surplus of able-bodied men. They are temporarily
withdrawn from the land, but the conditions are not ap-
preciably affected thereby. The crops are as well tended
as before; the economic waste involved lies in other directions.

LACK OF CREDITS

In case of a bad crop failure in most western countries,
it would be unusual if any large proportion of the people
were reduced to a state of famine. But in China the position
is just the reverse.

The plight of the Chinese farmer is due not alone to
poverty but to an even greater extent to the impossibility
of borrowing sufficient funds to tide over to the next harvest.
It is true that official loan regulations are often issued in

times of famine. In 1920–1921 a mandate was promulgated providing that the maximum interest rate should be three per cent monthly. The fact is, however, that this edict was not heeded, for cases are known where much higher rates, even as high as eight or nine per cent monthly, were charged. As a matter of fact, even the government itself, according to the Bureau of Economic Information, pays as high as 25 per cent interest for short-term loans.

Banks in China are comparatively few in number and are located, naturally, in the larger towns and cities. It is, therefore, difficult for the farmers to borrow from regular banking institutions. Sometimes grain dealers in the market towns carry on a loan business. They are usually more accessible to the country people than are the banks, they are better informed as to the credit of the borrower, and they can make collections more easily. Thus the borrower can obtain more favorable terms. Dearth of capital results in a phenomenally high interest rate. In normal years and with good security the rural bankers require from 20 to 36 per cent annually. In famine years the rate is much higher, often being more than 100 per cent. Even on such terms and with real property to hypothecate, it is often impossible for the farmers to contract a loan. The poor peasant has then to seek a pawnbroker or a money lender. If he is successful in his search he learns that the interest rates are higher still than with the banks and that he can borrow only up to one-half of the value of the real property he gives as security.

It is probably more usual for possessions to be sold outright in case of financial distress; but when a whole district is threatened with famine, it is impossible to find buyers, and then the poorest must literally sit down and starve.

Those who do not own land and who have only their small possessions to offer for security must resort to the pawnshop, which is a factor in China's economic life of far more importance than in the West. Here the loan is quickly made, and no questions are asked. But the rate of interest is high, and the term is short, generally ranging from four months to one year; and if the unfortunate man is unable to pay the loan when due he loses his property, although the loan may be but a fraction of the value of the security.

THE MONEY LENDER

To the very poor, who have no real property to pledge, there is left only the loan shark. If the borrowers have work or a reasonable prospect of regular income they can get an advance. The sums involved in such cases are usually small. The loan is generally made in coppers, and sometimes the repayment is called for in silver—a device often used to bewilder the ignorant and obscure the rate of interest. In the agreement no mention is made of the amount of the loan, the borrower agreeing to pay back a certain sum daily for a fixed number of days. Investigations recently made in Peking have shown that a rate as high as 40 per cent a month has been exacted.

But it must not be inferred that the money lender is totally bad. Times occur when only the help which he may be willing to extend will save a family from starvation. When it is considered that he receives no security for his advance and that installments must be collected at frequent intervals—an element of considerable expense to the lender—it appears that the rate exacted is, in many instances, not exorbitant. Although Great Britain has probably examined the possibilities of preventing abuses of usury as thoroughly as any other modern state, and although Parliament since the time of the Plantagenets has been passing legislation on the subject, the fact that bills have been presented in both Houses during the past year would indicate that no satisfactory remedy has yet been found. It is not possible to prohibit the practice of lending money by making it a criminal offense, for there is little distinction between legitimate banking and illegitimate money lending. However great the abuses connected with this business may be, and however desirable it may be to society that they should be abolished, there often arise urgent demands which can be met only by the money lender.

FIG. 15

FIG. 16

FIG. 17

FIG. 15—A Shantung village flooded by the Yellow River in 1925.

FIG. 16—The Yellow River flooded many hundreds of square miles of good farm land in 1925.

FIG. 17—Salvaging the crops from flooded fields in Shantung, 1925.

Loan Associations

With a wider knowledge of methods employed in other countries there has developed of late years an extension of money lending by means of Loan Associations. These are formed by the sale of shares of definite denomination bearing a specified rate of interest, usually 30 per cent per annum. The associations are usually organized for three years. They elect officers who supervise the transactions of the society. The officers receive no salary but are accorded one per cent commission on every transaction and a bonus on net earnings.

All loans granted must be guaranteed by a firm or individual of satisfactory financial standing. The interest rate fluctuates greatly, the loan agreement usually requiring the repayment of a sum 20 per cent greater than the face value of the loan. The method of amortization is by daily payments, and the term varies from four months to one year. If repayment must be completed in four months, interest is at the rate of 120 per cent per annum; while if the term is one year the rate is only 40 per cent. In addition to this two per cent of the face value of the loan is deducted for expenses of the association, and this increases the interest rate.

While banking facilities are not equal to those in other countries, there is one important factor peculiar to China which operates as a check upon borrowing. This is the family system requiring the pooling of resources. In this way the more prosperous members or branches of the family provide for the poorer relatives against temporary periods of unemployment, sickness, or loss of crops. This system applies not only to the immediate members of a family but also to its more distant branches. Thus a reserve is created which often makes outside help unnecessary.

Antiquated Agricultural Methods

The recurrence of famines in China and the severity of these disasters depend upon the amount of foodstuffs available to the population at any given time. Obviously antiquated methods of farming that tend to restrict production have an important bearing on this problem.

The great plains of China are intensively farmed. Owing to abundant labor and small individual holdings production is greater than for any similar area in the United States or other countries where labor is scarce and machine methods are employed. Chinese farmers through centuries of experience have developed methods of their own, and an appreciation of their tremendous accomplishments in the face of great odds may well precede any criticism. In the first place, simply because Chinese methods are old it should not be assumed that they are necessarily bad or that they fail to meet conditions of life in the Orient; rather the opposite. In fact, as Dr. F. H. King has well shown in his classic "Farmers of Forty Centuries,"[10] methods which have endured and been perfected through so long a time must have unusual merit. It has been clearly demonstrated that an exchange of ideas between China and other countries would bring great benefit to both. The belief that there is much to learn from China has prompted the United States Department of Agriculture to send experts there to gather information; but studies that have been made by universities in China and by Chinese students abroad have proved beyond doubt that there are many modern methods which might be adopted that would increase production in China.

MAINTENANCE OF SOIL FERTILITY

The greatest achievement of the Chinese farmer has been the maintenance of the fertility of the soil for four thousand years under a constant burden of intensive production. When it is considered that strong, virgin farm lands in America have been exhausted in three or four generations and that too without the tremendous pressure of population on subsistence prevailing in China, the magnitude of this accomplishment can be more heartily appreciated. The secret

[10] F. H. King: Farmers of Forty Centuries, 1911; new edit. in press.

of this success is largely in the Chinese method of fertilization, achieved entirely without the aid of chemical fertilizers. The wastes of the human body and the wastes of fuel are, after careful preparation taking several months, put back in the soil as manure.

Fig. 18—Primitive methods in China: a native rice huller.

Another great factor that has helped to keep the farm lands fertile has been their wide irrigation, particularly in central and southern China. This has not only brought water to the crops but has constantly replenished the fields with new exceptionally fertile soil precipitated from the flood waters of the many rivers.

Prevention of soil erosion of the cultivable lands has also been widely practiced, at tremendous expense in human labor but with results that have justified the outlay. Fields are so constructed as not only to avoid erosion but to catch the maximum amount of soluble and suspended matter in the run-off. Hillside fields have been terraced and carefully graded and bounded by raised rims which retain the run-off until suspended matter has settled.

The crops selected as staple are inherently adapted to the climate and soil of China. In central and southern China, where rain is abundant, the chief crop is rice. This crop permits the farmer to utilize as nearly as possible the total benefit from the heavy precipitation, as well as the run-off from adjacent uncultivated mountainous country. It is also a cereal that will stand intense fertilization. In the north, where rain is less and not so dependable, the drought-

FIG. 19—The native plow does not cut a deep furrow.

resisting millets are cultivated as well as wheat and kaoliang. Millet matures quickly, thrives in a hot climate, and grows vigorously in heavy rains. The planting of millet and wheat in hills or drills, instead of broadcasting it as in America, permits intertillage and tends to conserve the moisture of the soil.

INTENSIVE CULTIVATION

The practice of working over organic matter with soil or subsoil before it is applied to the fields, although requiring great labor, serves to lengthen the growing season and makes multiple cropping possible. Sometimes as many as three crops are grown simultaneously in one field, all being in different stages of development, one nearing maturity while another is just coming up. In this way the maximum efficiency of the soil is obtained.

Rice is started in hills and later transplanted spear by spear. This requires much labor, but enough plants are started on one acre to cover ten acres when transplanted; and while the rice is getting started on one acre the other nine acres are used for other crops which are harvested before the transplanting season.

These are some of the easily discernible reasons why China has been able to produce so much more abundantly than western countries and to sustain a population of more than four hundred million. But the splendid achievements of the past could have been improved upon in some ways, and these improvements would perhaps have helped to create a surplus of wealth which would make famines less likely. Some of the possibilities will be considered in Chapter V.

DEPLETION OF FORESTS

The barren eroded hills of China and the vast expanse of plain where the monotony of the scenery is broken only by occasional clumps of trees used for shade in the villages or maintained to mark the graves of the departed tell a heartbreaking story of the improvidence of man. The questions of the effect of the denuding of China's forests on erosion, the silting up of rivers, the regulation of rainfall, and other related topics will be discussed in Chapter II; but the economic effect of denudation may be briefly noted here.

Wood is one of the important material requirements of the modern state. It is absolutely essential to industry. China now finds herself on the threshold of industrial expansion; but she is devoid of forests and forest products in the very regions where the greatest development should and will take place. In Manchuria alone is there timber in any quantity. Even there the supply is in no way adequate to meet the demand, and transportation is so difficult that Oregon pine, imported from America, is used in preference to the native product.

Having lived so many centuries without forests the country people have probably arrived at a total lack of appreciation of their benefits. Those who do understand the value of trees and have undertaken to plant them have for the most part been disappointed. Trees have been carried away by neighboring farmers or appropriated by the soldiers for fuel; or financial reverses on the part of the owner have necessitated their sacrifice before they attained a size which would give the best economic return.

Poor Communications

The worst famine that has occurred in China within the memory of the present inhabitants is the great drought famine of 1876–1879. During these three years it was reported that practically no rain fell in the provinces of Shensi, Shansi, Chihli, Honan, and a part of Shantung, and reports of the Famine Relief Committees organized to bring help to the unfortunate victims state that from nine to thirteen millions of human beings perished from hunger, disease, or violence.

Although the immediate cause of this famine was the protracted drought, the reason for the tremendous death rate must be ascribed to lack of communications. In the first place, it took months for the news of the distress in the interior to reach the capital and ports. People were actually dying in great numbers over a wide area before any concerted action was taken to bring aid from the outside; and a disaster of such widespread proportions—the district affected covered about 300,000 square miles—soon exhausted the surplus of grain in the stricken provinces. Then, after conditions became known, the task of transporting the needed quantity of grain over a distance of several hundred miles without railways or improved roads presented a problem that could not be solved. The Chairman of the Foreign Relief Committee in Tientsin in his report said:

In November, 1877, the aspect of affairs was simply terrible. The autumn crops over the whole of Shansi and the greater part of Chihli, Honan, and Shensi had failed. . . . Tientsin was inundated with supplies from every available port. The Bund was piled mountain high with grain, the Government storehouses were full, all the boats were impressed for the conveyance of supplies towards Shansi and the Hochien districts of Chihli. Carts and wagons were all taken up and the cumbersome machinery of the Chinese Government was strained to the utmost to meet the enormous peril which stared it in the face. During the winter and spring of 1877–78, the most frightful disorder reigned supreme along the route to Shansi. Hwailu-hsien, the starting point was filled with officials and traders all intent on getting their convoys over the pass. Fugitives, beggars, and thieves absolutely swarmed. The officials were powerless to create any sort of order among the mountains. The track was completely worn out, and until a new one was made a dead block ensued. Camels, oxen, mules, and donkeys were hurried along in the wildest confusion, and so many perished or were killed by the desperate people in the hills, for the sake of their flesh, that the transit could only be carried on by the banded vigilance of the interested owners of grain, assisted by the train bands, or militia, which had been hastily got together, some of whom were armed with breech-loaders. . . . Night traveling was out of the question. The way was marked by the carcasses or skeletons of men and beasts, and the wolves, dogs, and foxes soon put an end to the sufferings of any wretch who lay down to recover from or die of his sickness in those terrible defiles. . . . Broken carts, scattered grain bags, dying men and animals so frequently stopped the way, that it was often necessary to prevent for days together the entry of convoys on the one side, in order to let the trains from the other come over. No idea of employing the starving people in making a new, or improving the old road ever presented itself to the authorities; and passengers, thankful for their escape from the dangers of the journey, were lost in wonder that the enormous traffic was possible.

In 1920–1921 almost analogous climatic conditions obtained throughout the same territory so badly hit forty-four years before. In the five northern provinces there was no rain for a year prior to the fall crop of 1920; but more rapid communications enabled the disaster to be anticipated, and as early as September, 1920, plans were being laid both by the Government and by philanthropic agencies to meet the distress.

During the interval of forty-four years since the previous great famine, something like 6000 miles of railways had been constructed in China. It will be seen from the accompanying map that these lines crossed or penetrated all the affected provinces except Shensi. It was this fact more than any other which made the immense relief operations possible and successful and which kept down the number of deaths to less than half a million.

FIG. 20

FIG. 21

FIG. 22

FIG. 20—The water buffalo of Central China makes a good draft animal.

FIG. 21—A native wheelbarrow in Hupeh.

FIG. 22—A Chinese cart. The narrow tires of these vehicles soon ruin the roads.

But the railways, while they were a tremendous help, were not adequate to meet the situation entirely. Manchuria had a good crop, and the stations along the Peking-Mukden Railway were filled with cereals awaiting shipment while people were starving only a few hundred miles away.

More is necessary than the provision of trunk railway lines. Foodstuffs must be transported from the railhead to interior points. Before the 1920 famine practically nothing had been done in China toward building roads suitable for motor truck or even for heavy cart traffic. The American Red Cross utilized its famine relief funds in Shantung and Shansi provinces in the payment of able-bodied famine victims on road work, and nearly 850 miles of highways were constructed in this way. Since 1920 several times as much mileage has been built by the China International Famine Relief Commission.

FIG. 23—The long hauls in China are made by water.

INEFFICIENT TRANSPORTATION METHODS

Only in the northern provinces are horse or mule-drawn vehicles widely used for transport. Over the greater part of the country the still more antique method of using animal or human carriers is followed. By far the greater portion of freight is moved by human labor; in some provinces wheelbarrows are used, in others no vehicle of any sort. This is the most inefficient mode that could be found, but the tremendous labor surplus has kept the practice alive.

It is interesting to note the limit to which this method of

transportation can be effective in bringing relief to a famine-stricken area. Mr. J. E. Baker, Adviser on Accounts and Statistics to the Chinese Ministry of Communications and a recognized authority on transportation matters in China, says:

A strong man can carry 100 catties (133 lbs.) on his back about 50 li (17 miles, or 26 kilometers) in a day. Averaging the effect of sickness, accidents, rough roads, and other disadvantageous circumstances, the average man's accomplishment would be considerably less than this. Probably about 17 kilometers would be nearer the average performance of the average man. One hundred catties is about one-seventeenth of a long ton. Hence, the average day's work for the average man is about one ton-kilometer per day. It is well known, of course, that for a few days under sufficient inducement a man can do much more than this. But the work of armies on the march proves that this figure is about correct.

Now a man carrying 100 catties on his back 17 kilometers during a day would need to eat about two catties of good, nourishing food. If the race of men is going to continue, he will also have to bring up a family. The average family consists of five members. They will have to eat. Suppose that the children and women folk each eat only one catty a day. That makes

Fig. 24—A strong man can carry 100 catties (133 lbs.) on his back.

four more catties that will have to be supplied for this carrier. His family will need some clothes, a little salt, and a few other bare necessities. Suppose the equivalent of one and a half catties be required for these other necessities. Then seven and a half catties will be consumed by the carrier and his family. A carrier taking grain to market, with his family, would consume the entire load in 13 days—six and a half days to market and as many days for the return. At 17 kilometers a day, the market could not be more than 111 kilometers distant, say 225 li (or 75 miles).[11]

In other words, the carrier and his dependents would

[11] J. E. Baker: The Economic Value of Railroad Transportation, *China Weekly Rev.*, Shanghai, Vol. 32, 1925.

consume the entire load in the time that it would take him
to penetrate 75 miles into the famine area, leave his burden,
and return home—supposing that he lived outside of the
famine belt and were unable to obtain a load for the return
trip. If there were freight to be moved back, this distance
could be correspondingly increased. If the transportation
were done by the famine sufferers themselves who reside
within the distressed region no better results could be expected, since for every able-bodied man who could be secured
as a carrier there would be on the average four dependents,
women, children, and aged. Relief cannot be brought,
therefore, to a district beyond fifty to one hundred miles
from the source of supply if the grain is carried. In localities
where the roads are serviceable for wheelbarrows this distance
can be increased two and one-half times.

WATER TRANSPORT

In actual practice the long hauls are made by water, and
human carriers work from the waterways inland and in the
hilly country where the rivers are not navigable even for
small craft. The early development of canals shows that
the benefits to be derived from water transport have been
appreciated for many centuries. Thousands of miles of
canals have been constructed, the best known being the Grand
Canal which extends from Peking to Hangchow. This
waterway was begun in 540 B. C., but it has greatly dete-
riorated of late years through the migrations of the Yellow
River. Transportation by water is very slow, for steamboats
are scarcely used except on the Yangtze and a few other
rivers. The great volume of traffic is handled by man
power, the small cargo boats being poled or towed, except
when a favorable wind or current furnishes a brief respite
to the crew from their arduous labors. So, for purposes of
relief in times of disaster the present transportation practices
in China are far from satisfactory, and the lack of adequate
communications results in great distress. Local famines
are of perennial occurrence in isolated districts simply because

of lack of facilities for bringing in grain from near-by centers where a surplus is available. Residents in one province may be dying from starvation while adjoining provinces on either side are having excellent crops.

There are no statistics that give even a general idea of the volume of freight transported every year in China except for that small portion carried by the railways. Mr. J. E. Baker estimates that the freight moved last year on the 7500 miles of railways if handled by man power would have required 25,000,000 men on the basis of a daily ton-kilometer haul. In the United States there are approximately 260,000 miles of railways, and on the same basis 1,250,000,000 men would have been needed to transport the freight carried during the same twelve months. Such figures show in a striking way not only the difference between the two countries in the development of railroad transportation but the difference in the standard of living.

FIG. 25—The city of Hsin An, Chihli, surrounded by flood waters, 1924.

CHAPTER II

NATURAL CAUSES OF FAMINE

While the fundamental causes of famine are traceable to the economic circumstances in which the people live, the immediate cause is usually the result of some natural phenomenon. We are prone to associate the idea of serious food shortage with protracted droughts, swarms of locusts, widespread floods, or other visitations of nature's wrath, perhaps even to the extent of minimizing the part played by social, political, and economic factors. This is to be expected, since it is the spectacular or bizarre that is considered by the press to be of the greatest human interest and since it is through the newspapers that we learn of the world's affairs. Thus the appalling situation of the millions of Chinese who live along the Yellow River, a situation which assures actual starvation for great numbers upon the loss of even one crop, will receive scant mention in the world's news until a flood pushes them over the edge into the abyss of famine.

But there are some famines that are due almost solely to natural causes, and there are scarcely any to which natural phenomena do not contribute. Probably in no other country —certainly in no other country of its size or of anything like its population—are the natural features less favorable to the inhabitants than in China. The mass of the people live on the great alluvial plains traversed by meandering rivers, very few of which have well defined channels. The rainfall is very irregular, especially in the north. Long periods of drought are frequent when the crops are a total

36

failure; severe floods occur when the rivers break their dikes and inundate thousands of square miles of farm lands, destroying the growing foodstuffs in addition to causing loss of life and doing great damage to property.

DEFORESTATION

Scientists ascribe these conditions or their augmentation to the depletion of China's forests by successive generations of inhabitants. It is believed that the area now constituting China proper was once heavily wooded, and there seem to be ample historical and geological proofs of this theory.

The contrast between present and former conditions in Shansi has been recently described by Professor Lowdermilk[12] of Nanking University, who studied on the spot the processes of converting a forest cover to denuded slopes. Nine-tenths of Shansi is mountainous, and over most of the slope area a gradient of 25 per cent obtains. Under the torrential thunderstorm type of rainfall the unprotected surface is rapidly destroyed. In northern Shansi the soil layer is removed in three to ten years. Referring to the former extent of forest, Professor Lowdermilk says: "Perhaps the most trustworthy indications are the existing temple forests. To include all areas of similar altitude, or higher, with the existing temple forests would in itself indicate an extensive forest cover for Shansi."

We are not concerned here with the reasons for the destruction of this great resource. It is enough to know that the actions of former generations have resulted in a deforestation more complete than that of any other great nation. Not only has deforestation had much to do in bringing about present conditions, but it is generally believed that a gradual drying up of the areas in the north and west is taking place and that more and more of the present fertile country will become arid like the regions of Central Asia, and for the same reason.

[12] W. C. Lowdermilk: Forest Destruction and Slope Denudation in the Province of Shansi, *China Journ. of Sci. and Arts*, Vol. 4, 1926, pp. 127–135.

Drought: Historical Data

Without doubt the worst famines in China have been caused by a lack of sufficient rainfall for a long period. Lack of rain occurs most often in northern and central China. While most other natural disasters result in only a partial destruction of the crops, a drought makes of a normally flourishing countryside a barren waste. When it is remembered that in China almost the entire population exists by agriculture, it can be imagined what effect a dry period has, especially if it continues for two or three years, as sometimes happens. In time of drought it is only in those districts where irrigation is practiced that any crop at all can be harvested, and unfortunately these districts are too few in number and small in extent.

In 1878 Alexander Hosie, of the British Consular Service in China, compiled from the mass of historical and statistical data contained in the great Chinese compendium known as the T'u Shu Tsih Ch'eng a record of the droughts which occurred in China from the commencement of the T'ang Dynasty in A.D. 620 to the end of the Ming Dynasty in 1643.[13] More recently a compilation from the beginning of the Christian era up to the end of the last century has been made by Dr. Co-Ching Chu, of the National Southeastern University, Nanking.[14] While these two compilations are not in entire harmony—for the records, themselves obviously neither complete nor exact, are open to different interpretations—they give the best available information on the history of droughts.

Mr. Hosie finds that in the millennium from 620 to 1619 there were recorded 610 years when one or more of the provinces had insufficient rain, and in 203 years great or very severe drought is specified. Probably in those years the distress was sufficient to cause famines of some magnitude, and that extremely severe food shortage was experienced

[13] Alexander Hosie: Droughts in China, A. D. 620 to 1643, *Journ. North China Branch of the Royal Asiatic Soc.*, Vol. 12 (N. S.), 1878, pp. 51–89.
[14] Co-Ching Chu: Climatic Pulsations During Historic Time in China, *Geogr. Rev.*, Vol. 16, 1926, pp. 274–282.

FIG. 26

FIG. 27

FIG. 26—The floods in Hunan in 1924 were the most destructive experienced for fifty years.

FIG. 27—Havoc left in the wake of the Hunan flood of 1924.

during at least 15 of the worst years is indicated by an allusion to cannibalism in the Chinese records. It is interesting to note that cannibalism is mentioned as having occurred most often in Shensi, less frequently in Honan, Shansi, and Shantung, and only once or twice in provinces farther south. The great famines occurred when the droughts were of long duration or when the area affected was large. The province of Chekiang is recorded as having suffered for the six successive years 1170 to 1175 and the four successive years 1180 to 1183. Instances when two or more provinces were simultaneously affected for several successive years, though uncommon, are not rare. For example Chihli and Honan were both affected during the period 1296 to 1298 and in the five consecutive years 1324 to 1328. For the three years 990 to 992 the three provinces of Chihli, Honan, and Shensi are recorded as having suffered simultaneously. Chihli, Honan, Shansi, and Shantung have most frequently had droughts simultaneously or in successive years. This fact, coupled with the more frequent mention of cannibalism in the northern provinces and with the fact that of the 216 great droughts 100 were in the provinces of Chihli, Honan, Shansi, Shantung, and Shensi, leads indisputably to the conclusion that it is this part of China north of the Yangtze valley and extending to the boundary of Mongolia where a chronic drought condition exists (compare Fig. 4).

Table I, prepared from Mr. Hosie's paper, shows the number of occurrences of drought in each province in hundred-year periods, from A. D. 620 to 1619. For convenience in comparison the provinces of northern, central, and southern China are separated. In the northern group 100 of the droughts were listed as great, or very severe, in the central group 77, and in the southern group 39.

Table II, of droughts per century from the beginning of the Tang Dynasty to the beginning of the twentieth century, is taken from Dr. Chu's paper.

In considering these figures it must be borne in mind that droughts in China have been catalogued by the historians in terms of the suffering of the people. No measured rainfall

Table I—Droughts in the Districts now Constituting the Provinces of China Proper Arranged in 100-Year Periods from A. D. 620 to 1619

Province	620 to 719	720 to 819	820 to 919	920 to 1019	1020 to 1119	1120 to 1219	1220 to 1319	1320 to 1419	1420 to 1519	1520 to 1619	Totals
Northern Division											
Honan	4	6	4	41	17	1	12	18	4	5	112
Chihli	4	2	1	8	10	7	32	16	11	6	97
Shensi	11	8	7	11	8	8	9	10	9	10	91
Shansi	5	3	2	3	4	3	15	7	12	24	78
Shantung	5	2	1	3	7	9	13	7	8	6	61
Kansu	—	—	—	—	—	—	3	1	—	—	4
	29	21	15	66	46	28	84	59	44	51	443
Central Division											
Chekiang	—	3	6	3	8	31	5	15	18	24	113
Kiangsu	3	6	8	8	13	26	10	10	5	5	94
Hupeh	2	3	1	4	2	12	4	10	21	23	82
Szechwan	6	—	—	—	2	17	—	6	2	2	35
Anhwei	1	2	2	3	1	6	3	4	3	3	28
	12	14	17	18	26	92	22	45	49	57	352
Southern Division											
Kiangsi	—	2	4	5	4	19	4	5	7	9	59
Hunan	2	3	1	4	3	10	5	7	15	6	56
Fukien	—	1	1	—	3	8	5	3	9	18	48
Kwangsi	—	—	—	1	—	1	2	6	3	6	19
Yunnan	—	—	—	—	—	—	—	1	3	15	19
Kweichow	—	—	—	—	—	—	—	—	—	4	4
Kwangtung	—	1	—	—	—	1	4	2	3	4	15
	2	7	6	10	10	39	20	24	40	62	220
Grand Totals	43	42	38	94	82	159	126	128	133	170	1015

records were kept, and it was only when crops failed and starvation conditions occurred that drought was recognized as drought. Hence it is natural that the more densely populated provinces such as Kiangsu, Chekiang, Honan, and Chihli occur most often in the records, for here a lack of rain and the failure of the crops would most quickly bring about a state of famine. Furthermore, as Dr. Chu points out and as the paucity of records from Kansu would suggest, droughts in places a short distance from the capital of the empire attract more notice than those at a distance.

Again, mention is frequently made in the Chinese histories of a great drought and the remission of taxes. It has been

TABLE II—NUMBER OF DROUGHTS PER CENTURY OBSERVED DURING
DIFFERENT DYNASTIES IN CHINESE HISTORY

DYNASTY	TANG	FIFTH DYNASTY AND NORTH SUNG	SOUTH SUNG	YUEN	MING	MANCHU
Christian Era	618–907	908–1126	1127–1279	1280–1367	1368–1643	1644–1847 1861–1900
Capital	Chang-an Shensi	Kai-fung Honan	Hangchow Chekiang	Peking Chihli	Peking Chihli	Peking Chihli
Honan . . .	4.2	24.2	5.3	21.9	2.9	12.4
Chihli . . .	2.1	9.1	9.9	29.9	5.1	26.9
Shensi . . .	4.5	6.9	5.3	12.7	7.3	9.5
Shansi . . .	4.5	2.3	5.3	19.6	13.8	7.3
Shangtung. .	3.4	3.7	6.6	8.1	4.0	19.0
Kansu . . .	0.4	1.4	0.7	5.8	0.7	7.0
Chekiang . .	3.1	4.1	15.2	6.9	16.7	13.9
Kiangsu. . .	4.2	4.1	14.5	10.4	3.3	15.7
Hupeh . . .	1.7	2.3	4.6	12.7	16.0	11.2
Szechwan . .	1.7	—	9.2	2.3	1.5	0.4
Anhwei . .	4.5	7.8	9.9	4.6	2.2	14.5
Kiangsi . .	1.7	0.9	6.6	3.5	4.4	13.6
Hunan . . .	1.7	2.7	4.0	6.9	5.1	8.7
Fukien . . .	1.4	1.4	5.9	4.6	7.6	3.7
Kwangsi . .	—	0.5	—	6.9	4.7	2.1
Yunnan . .	—	—	—	—	6.5	0.8
Kweichow. .	—	—	—	—	1.1	—
Kwangtung .	—	—	1.3	4.6	2.9	0.8

customary in China as a relief measure to remit taxes in
areas that have suffered some major catastrophe. But
ofttimes a distress of small proportions has been magnified
by the officials of the provinces simply as a measure to obtain
from the throne the remission of the taxes. This has probably
led to the inclusion of droughts that were not serious. The
writer is of the opinion that for this reason the figures for
Kiangsu and Chekiang and perhaps some of the other central or southern densely populated and influential provinces
are too large.

RAINFALL OF CHINA

The northern provinces, where droughts are most frequent
and most severe, depend upon the summer monsoons for
their rainfall. In normal years there is ample precipitation
in June, July, and August, a slight snowfall occasionally

TABLE III—NUMBER OF FLOODS PER CENTURY OBSERVED DURING
DIFFERENT DYNASTIES IN CHINESE HISTORY

DYNASTY	TANG	FIFTH DYNASTY AND NORTH SUNG	SOUTH SUNG	YUEN	MING	MANCHU
Christian Era	*618–907*	*908–1126*	*1127–1279*	*1280–1367*	*1368–1643*	*1644–1847 1861–1900*
Capital	*Chang-an Shensi*	*Kai-fung Honan*	*Hangchow Chekiang*	*Peking Chihli*	*Peking Chihli*	*Peking Chihli*
Honan . . .	4.2	17.8	1.3	34.4	2.2	26.0
Chihli . . .	2.1	6.9	3.9	25.3	1.8	43.7
Shensi . . .	9.1	1.8	3.9	4.6	2.2	11.6
Shansi . . .	0.7	2.3	—	4.6	7.3	12.3
Shangtung .	1.7	5.5	0.7	20.7	2.2	27.7
Kansu . . .	0.3	1.8	1.3	5.7	—	8.3
Chekiang . .	1.4	1.4	17.8	4.6	4.0	22.7
Kiangsu . .	1.4	2.7	9.9	3.4	1.5	43.8
Hupeh . . .	0.3	0.9	4.6	4.6	0.7	26.2
Szechwan . .	0.7	—	2.6	—	1.1	2.9
Anhwei . .	0.7	3.7	5.9	4.6	—	36.3
Kiangsi . .	0.7	1.4	5.9	4.6	1.5	21.8
Hunan . . .	—	1.4	—	3.4	1.1	20.6
Fukien . . .	—	0.9	4.6	4.6	3.3	6.5
Kwangsi . .	—	0.5	—	1.2	0.7	1.6
Yunnan . .	—	—	—	—	6.9	2.5
Kweichow .	—	—	—	—	—	2.5
Kwangtung .	—	0.5	0.7	2.3	1.5	7.0

during the winter, and showers in April and May. Perhaps
it would be better to say that this is the ideal year rather
than the normal, for it is not often that the showers occur
at the planting season in April and May, and many times
the winter wheat is not favored with snowfall. The total
annual rainfall is not large. Hann gives 21 inches as an
average for northern China, 70 per cent of which falls in
the three months of June, July, and August. The principal
crops in the north are wheat, which is harvested in June, and
millet and kaoliang, which are gathered in September. If
the snows and early spring showers fail, there is a small
wheat crop; and if the summer rains likewise do not occur,
there is no harvest for the entire year.

Although the northern and central parts of the country are
more susceptible to drought, it occasionally occurs in the
more southern provinces; but usually it does not affect so

great an area. In the central and southern provinces the principal crop, rice, requires a great deal of moisture.

BREAKING A DROUGHT

The ancient Chinese methods of breaking a drought are interesting, and they are probably as effective as any discovered in the West. When matters really become serious the governors of the provinces concerned issue mandates forbidding the slaughter of live stock, and the population goes without meat for three days. If this does not bring the desired rain, processions are formed, and a sort of holiday is declared in order to invoke the heavens. In Hantan, Chihli Province, there is an iron tablet which has most wonderful properties for bringing rain. In 1924 there was a very dry spring, and the summer monsoon did not arrive in June as it should. Matters finally reached such a pass that the Central Government in desperation decided to bring the iron tablet to Peking from the country. This was done in July, and lo, the heavens opened, and China had one of the worst floods of several decades.

Before the overthrow of the monarchy the responsibility for breaking protracted droughts rested with the Emperor, since it was his duty to importune the heavens on behalf of the people. The prayer of Tao Kwang for rain which was made in 1832 is a splendid example of a memorial on this subject of drought. The following translation is taken from "The Middle Kingdom" by S. Wells Williams.

Oh, alas! imperial Heaven, were not the world afflicted by extraordinary changes, I would not dare to present extraordinary services. But this year the drought is most unusual. Summer is past, and no rain has fallen. Not only do agriculture and human beings feel the dire calamity, but also beasts and insects, herbs and trees, almost cease to live. I, the minister of Heaven, am placed over mankind, and am responsible for keeping the world in order and tranquillizing the people. Although it is now impossible for me to sleep or eat with composure, although I am scorched with grief and tremble with anxiety, still, after all, no genial and copious showers have been obtained.

Some days ago I fasted, and offered rich sacrifices on the altars of the gods of the land and the grain, and had to be thankful for gathering clouds and slight showers; but not enough to cause gladness. Looking up, I consider that Heaven's heart is benevolence and love. The sole cause is the daily deeper atrocity of my sins; but little sincerity and little devotion. Hence I have been unable to move Heaven's heart, and bring down abundant blessings. . . .

Prostrate I beg imperial Heaven (*Hwang Tien*) to pardon my ignorance and stupidity, and to grant me self-renovation; for myriads of innocent people are involved by me, the One man. My sins are so numerous it is difficult to escape from them. Summer is past and autumn arrived; to wait longer will really be impossible. Knocking head, I pray imperial Heaven to hasten and confer gracious deliverance—a speedy and divinely beneficial rain, to save the people's lives and in some degree redeem my iniquities. Oh, alas! imperial Heaven, observe these things. Oh, alas! imperial Heaven, be gracious to them. I am inexpressibly grieved, alarmed, and frightened. Reverently this memorial is presented.[15]

Flood Occurrence

Floods occur in all sections of the country but in some parts more frequently and seriously (compare Table III, p. 43). The greatest number of floods occur in the provinces of Chihli, Shantung, Honan, Kiangsu, Anhwei, and Chekiang. Parts of all these provinces lie in the great eastern plain, which has been built up of recent river deposits. The great plain is practically level for immense distances, and the streams are held in their courses by means of earthen dikes, most of which were built hundreds of years ago. The country is so flat that when the dikes give way a tremendous area is flooded, and unfortunately this is almost always the district that is the most thickly settled and under the most intensive cultivation.

Most of the rivers carry a great quantity of silt which slowly builds up the stream bed, necessitating the constant raising of the dikes. Eventually a point is reached where even the bed of the river is above the land outside the dikes. As L. H. Dudley Buxton has well put it, the rivers are *on* the plain, not *in* it.[16] This is the reason why the heavy silt-laden rivers have changed their courses so often, for when

[15] S. Wells Williams: The Middle Kingdom (revised edit., 2 vols., New York, 1883), Vol. 1, p. 467.

[16] L. H. D. Buxton: The Eastern Road, London and New York, 1924.

the dikes fail the entire stream abandons its old bed for the lower country, and the task of forcing the flow back into its original channel presents too great a problem for the crude methods of the people.

It is the frequent inundation of the plains that has made them so level, for the immense quantity of silt, which but for the floods would have been carried by the streams to the sea, has been deposited over the country. This process, repeated many times during thousands of years, has tended to fill the depressions and slowly to build up new land. As the process has gone on the gradient of the streams has been constantly decreased with corresponding lessening of their ability to carry their load of mud to the sea. One beneficial effect can be credited to the frequent floods in the plains. The new earth deposited is extremely rich, and this constant acquisition of virgin soil has helped to keep up the productivity of the country.

Slow Drainage of Flood Waters

The immediate loss of life and property is not the only terrible aspect of a flood, but also the wholesale destruction of the growing crops and the slow drainage which often prevents the next planting. In some regions it takes as much as two or three years for the waters of a severe inundation to find their way to the sea. This slow drainage, while due in part to the level nature of the country, is probably influenced to a greater extent by the network of dikes built along the streams and canals. These hold back the flood waters until their volume overtops the dikes, or the latter are breached by wave action, and then the water rushes on until it reaches the next obstruction. Naturally every effort is made by the natives, who are protected by these dikes, to postpone the evil day when their own fields will be covered with water, and they carefully patrol them to prevent the inhabitants of inundated districts from making breaches to hasten the draining of their own land.

The lack of forest cover on the hills results in an extremely rapid run-off; and this, coupled with the torrential rains

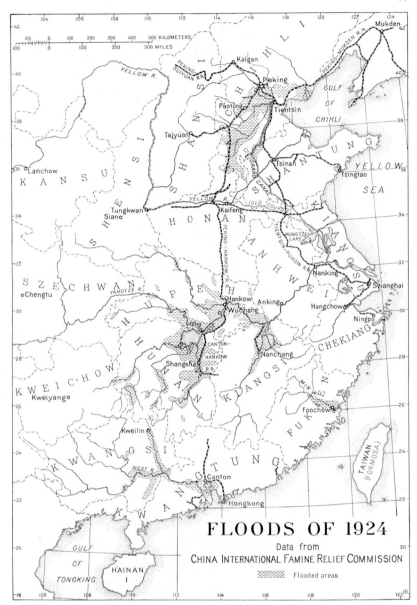

FIG. 28—Map showing the flooded areas in 1924. Scale 1 : 17,500,000.

liable to occur in almost any part of the country, transforms even dry stream beds into raging torrents within a very brief time. Although these conditions are prevalent in nearly all the provinces, there are certain districts where the configuration of the land and the nature of the rivers cause disasters of especial severity and frequency.

THE HWAI RIVER

The first in importance, from the point of view of crop losses and resultant famine distress, is in the valley of the Hwai in the provinces of Anhwei and Kiangsu. The Hwai River, which rises in Honan and flows through Anhwei into Kiangsu, has no regular channel to the sea but has emptied into Hungtze Lake since the Yellow River in 1191 burst its banks and usurped the original channel of the Hwai. In normal years when the rainfall is not too great and is sufficiently distributed the result of the summer rains is simply to raise the water level in the lake and perhaps to inundate a stretch of country contiguous to its boundary, the flood waters finding their way to the sea through the Grand Canal and the Yangtze River. But when the rainfall is unusually heavy, as happens every few years, the capacity of the lake is not sufficient as a ponding basin. Mr. John R. Freeman, the eminent American hydraulic engineer, after a brief examination of this problem reported as follows:

. . . Although much of this area is flat and absorptive, floods sometimes run off this large area into the vast, shallow Hungtze Lake at a rate of more than 200,000 cubic feet per second, as estimated from flood marks established by the American Red Cross engineers in 1914, and even reached the rate of 440,000 cubic feet per second in the exceptionally high flood of 1916, as measured by the engineers of the Kiang-Hwai Board.

Neither the St. Lawrence River at Montreal, nor the Mississippi River above the entrance of the Missouri, at its greatest flood period carries so high a rate of discharge.

The Hungtze Lake acts as a great natural equalizer and its outflow is somewhat controlled by sluiceways; but the flood trying to escape therefrom is pent in on the north by a broad ridge of sediment and dikes pertaining to the abandoned Yellow River channel and is held back on the east by the embankments on the Grand Canal, which to the limit of its capacity strives to lead the flood south to the Yangtze River, in which it is somewhat aided by the flow to the Yangtze through a chain of lakes.

These great floods give more than the channels can accommodate and they rupture the Grand Canal dikes, but even when the flood breaks over and sweeps away this barrier, its free escape seaward over the vast, low-lying area of more than fifty miles wide by one hundred miles long, is barred by the great Maritime Dike, known as the Fan Kung Dike, which was built about 900 years ago to protect this low-lying region from the sea.

The vast network of large and small canals within this area and the sluiceways through the Maritime Dike, all in combination, are utterly insufficient to safely or promptly discharge such a flood.[17]

After the flood of 1911 with its resulting immense loss of life and property, the American Red Cross, under an arrangement with the Chinese government, sent a Board of Engineers headed by Colonel William L. Sibert to investigate the Hwai River Con-

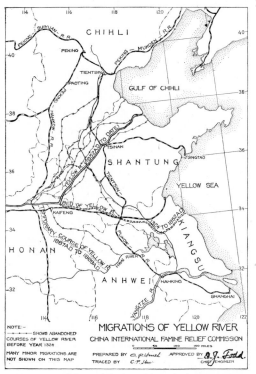

FIG. 29—Map showing historical migrations of the Yellow River.

servancy Project. In its report this Board stated that the last flood had inundated 10,470 square miles in Anhwei and 2300 square miles in Kiangsu and that these provinces are subject to a disaster of equal severity on the average once every six or seven years and a disaster of minor importance every three or four years. This area, larger than Belgium, comprises some of the best farming land in all China.

[17] See J. R. Freeman: Flood Problems in China, *Trans. Amer. Soc. of Civil Engineers*, Vol. 85, 1922, pp. 1405–1460.

Assuming that the normal yield of rice is 2000 pounds
an acre, the loss due to one of these serious floods is more
than 16,000,000,000 pounds; and, counting the less severe
inundations, probably 3,000,000,000 pounds of China's
principal food is destroyed annually as a result of these catastrophes.   This is sufficient to feed more than 6,000,000

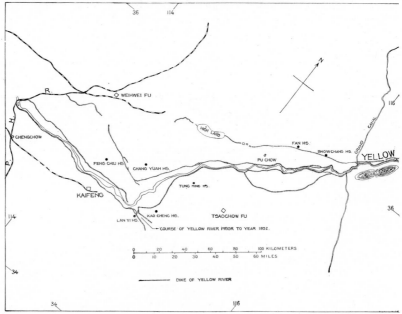

FIG. 30—Dike system of the lower course of the Yellow River.   Scale approximately 1 : 3,000,000.

adults.   Allowing for the children, more than 7,000,000 of
the population could be supported from this annual wastage.
Coupled with the damage occasioned by the years of
high water is the loss that results from the lack of drainage
of Hungtze Lake and the other low-lying regions.   It is
estimated that more than 600,000 acres could be reclaimed
if the proper conservancy scheme were carried out.   This
would mean an increase of more than 1,200,000,000 pounds
of rice annually—sufficient to feed a population of nearly
3,000,000.   In other words the total annual loss to the

country from this uncontrolled river is sufficient to provide food for approximately 10,000,000 people.

THE YELLOW RIVER

The Hwang Ho, or Yellow River, "China's Sorrow," seems to have been a problem since the dawn of history.

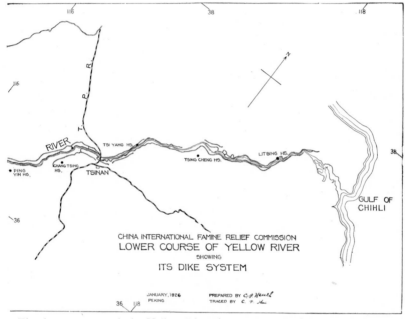

The lower course of the Yellow River has constantly fluctuated. Compare Figure 29.

The earliest annals give accounts of great inundations and of efforts to control the ravages of this menace. It is difficult to present an idea of the extent of the damage caused by the Yellow River floods. They occur at present less often than along the Hwai, and the area affected varies in extent from a few to many thousand square miles. The river has been meandering back and forth for thousands of years, as can be seen from the extent of the delta built up. It is not possible to trace all the courses of the river even in historic time, but the accompanying map (Fig. 29) is prepared from the most authentic material so far available. The Yellow River has flowed into the sea as far north as Tientsin, and its most southerly outlet was probably through the Yangtze River at Shanghai.

While floods of relatively minor importance occur as often as once or twice in every decade, there have been but three great migrations of the river in the past thousand years. On several occasions, however, there have been extremely severe floods when the river has left its course but later returned to its old bed. Such an instance is the flood of 1887–1889 when a break occurred in the southern dike in the province of Honan. According to Chinese official records more than 2,000,000 people lost their lives either from drowning or from starvation during the resulting famine, and nearly the whole province of Honan south of the river was inundated.

It is not only in times of unusually high water that there is danger of flood along the Yellow River. The distance between the dikes is great, and this permits of considerable meandering so that the current is constantly shifting from side to side. Hence when the river is rising the current may suddenly swing in toward a dike in an unprotected stretch, which, unless rapid and adequate measures are taken, soon crumbles away. This is what happened in Shantung Province in the summer and fall of 1925 when the southern dike was breached and an area of about 800 square miles was flooded. The loss in crops alone was estimated at $20,000,000, and yet the river was not at an unusually high stage when the disaster occurred.

THE RIVERS OF CHIHLI PROVINCE

There are eight principal rivers entering the Chihli plain. In ancient times these streams reached the sea through many channels. But when the Grand Canal was extended from the Yellow River to Tientsin in the thirteenth century no crossings were provided, or if provided were not maintained, and the waters were all led into the Hai Ho, which flows through Tientsin. This was already the outlet for the Pei Ho and the Yung Ting Ho, and its capacity has not been sufficient to carry off the flood waters in years when the rainfall has been heavy. Since 1891 there have been seven serious inundations of the central Chihli plain. It would therefore appear that this district is subject to floods on the average once every six or seven years. The total catchment area is more than 88,000 square miles; and when it is considered that all but a very small part of this water must reach the sea through the Hai Ho, a small stream, it can be understood why these disasters occur. The last serious Chihli flood was in the summer of 1924. During the severe storms in July it was estimated that the inflow into the river system was 25 times as great as the outflow through the Hai Ho. The difficulty of obtaining accurate reports simultaneously from various sections of the province makes it impossible to state exactly what extent of country was inundated at any one time; but it has been reliably established that an area of no less than 5000 square miles was covered with water long enough to destroy completely the growing crop which should have been harvested in September and October and that a large portion of this area was still inundated during the autumn, thus preventing the planting of the winter wheat. The lower section of the plain is but a little above sea level, and it usually takes two or three years for all the flood waters to reach the ocean.

If the value of the crop be put at only $30 an acre, the loss to the province was nearly $100,000,000, Chinese currency, simply from the destruction of growing foodstuffs. When to this are added the losses due to failure to plant the winter wheat and subsequent crops the sum will exceed $125,000,000. As such a catastrophe happens on the average every six or seven years, it may be estimated that the annual loss from these floods is not less than $18,000,000. This sum is sufficient to provide a livelihood for 120,000 families, or more than 600,000 people, according to the standard of living now prevailing in northern China. Nor must one overlook the loss from demolition of buildings and the

FIG. 31

FIG. 32

FIG. 33

FIG. 31—In its upper reaches the Yellow River flows through hilly country.
FIG. 32—Tungkwan, below which the Yellow River enters on its lower course.
FIG. 33—The lower Yellow River is confined between dikes some of which are
stone-faced.

FIG. 34

FIG. 35

FIG. 36

FIG. 34—Break of a Kan River dike, Kiangsi, probably because of lack of proper upkeep.

FIG. 35—Break of a Yellow River dike in Shantung, 1925.

FIG. 36—One of the dike breaks that caused the Chihli floods of 1924.

drowning of live stock and of human beings. In 1917 the dikes which protect Tientsin gave way, and damage to the extent of many millions of dollars was done in the city itself. In 1924 a similar catastrophe was narrowly averted: the principal seaport of northern China stands in constant danger of inundation with each successive flood.

In the Kan River delta region of Kiangsi Province large areas between the various mouths of the river and around the Poyang Lake have been diked in and produce a good yield of rice annually. In the 1924 floods most of these dikes were breached, and hundreds of square miles of good farming land were covered with water.

It is not intended to discuss here all the areas of China subject to floods; in fact, there is not sufficient dependable information concerning many of them to make it possible to give more than a general indication of the damage wrought by inundations. The specific examples given have been selected because in their case more reliable data are available and because they are the most frequently or most severely affected. If a thorough tabulation of the annual loss due to this cause could be made, the sum arrived at would reach a staggering total. In 1922–1923 there was a severe flood of the Tsao Ngo River in Chekiang. In 1924 central China was visited by the worst inundation recorded in many years, and large areas in Hunan, Hupeh, and Kiangsi were covered with water by an overflow of the Siang, the Kan, and the Yangtze Rivers. The same year saw a serious flood of the West River in Kwangsi and of the Min River in Fukien, as well as the flood in Chihli already mentioned. Other areas where floods occur include the basins of the following rivers: the Fen (Shansi), the Han (Hupeh), the Pearl (Kwangtung), the Liao (Manchuria), and the Min (Fukien).

Mention has already been made of the terraces on the hillsides, built by the labor of centuries. In the torrential rains that occur every few years these hillside fields are sometimes destroyed over wide areas. In the hilly region of southwestern Chihli during the storms of 1924, 23 inches of rain fell in 33 hours at one place, and other places registered

FIG. 37

FIG. 38

FIG. 37—A typical dike break. Chihli flood of 1924. (Photograph by Lawrence Impey.)

FIG. 38—When the dikes break, immense areas are flooded. (Photograph by W. H. Mallory.)

18 inches in 32 hours and 9 inches in 9 hours. No wonder that the fields are washed away. In some districts the destruction from this cause is so complete that whole villages are forced to seek new homes.

Then again, rich farming country near the foothills is ofttimes destroyed by the flooding of the streams which carry with them not only coarse sand and pebbles but also small boulders. There are places where such a heavy deposit of sand and stones is left on the fields after a flood season that they have to be abandoned. The loss from this source in Chekiang Province during the 1922 floods was very large.

THE LOCUST PEST

Locusts are one of the three principal natural causes of famine. This pest, which consumes the growing crops, leaves the countryside as barren as a protracted drought. While these insects are essentially herbivorous, they are known to attack and absolutely ruin even the trees; in this respect they are more damaging than a lack of rain.

Many stories are told of the countless numbers of locusts composing a migration. They always move in the daytime, and sometimes the swarms are so dense as to shut out completely the light of the sun. One invasion in Russia is said to have occupied an area twenty miles both in length and in breadth. In addition to the distress which follows the destruction of their crops, the people of a locust-infected district are ofttimes subjected to epidemics caused by the decayed insects getting into wells, cisterns, and reservoirs and clogging the drains, thus poisoning the drinking water.

There is no continent and almost no part of the world that has not been visited at one time or another by this scourge: only the arctic regions appear to be immune. But it is especially the territories between latitude 20° and 45° N. and between 15° and 45° S. that suffer most from locusts.[18]

In his paper on calamities M. Raoul Montandon, President of the Geographical Society of Geneva, lists the major dis-

[18] Paul Vayssière: Le problème acridien et sa solution internationale, *Matériaux pour l'Étude des Calamités*, Geneva, Vol. 1, 1924, pp. 122–158 and 274–282.

asters that have followed invasions of locusts, beginning from the year 125 B. C.[19] In this list China appears but three times, namely in the years 1835, 1878, and 1892. The failure to include catastrophes which occurred prior to the nineteenth century was probably due to the lack of intercourse between China and the West in former times which made reliable data difficult to obtain. The 162 famines recorded in the Chinese historical records for Shensi Province include 20 which were caused, in whole or in part, by locusts.

Alexander Hosie in his studies of the Chinese histories already referred to mentions visitations of locusts in the following provinces and years between A. D. 620 and 1643: 840 (Fukien); 869; 953; 991 (Shantung); 1016 (Chihli and Honan); 1027 (Shensi and Honan); 1033; 1053; 1128; 1176 (North China); 1215 (Central China); 1240 (Kiangsi); 1298 (Kiangsu); 1310 (North China); 1326 (Kwangsi); 1330 (Hunan); 1334 (Central China); 1541 (Chihli); 1581 (Chekiang); 1605 and 1640 (Chekiang).

It would seem from the above list that while locusts have visited nearly all parts of the country it is the central and northern provinces that have been most often attacked by the scourge.

The available information would indicate that locusts have not caused such serious disasters in China as in other countries subject to their depredations. Rather they have served to aggravate bad conditions due to other causes. This is notably the case in the visitation of 1878, which followed two years of drought in northern China. It must also be remembered that the northern Chinese are accustomed to eating locusts, a practice which would in some degree recompense the farmers for the losses sustained by the action of the insects on the crops.

Earthquakes

Although China lies outside the great earthquake zones of the world (the Pacific girdle and the Mediterranean-Himala-

[19] Raoul Montandon: À propos du projet Ciraolo: Une carte mondiale de distribution géographique des calamités, *Rev. Internatl. de la Croix-Rouge*, Geneva, Vol. 5, 1923, pp. 271–344.

yan belt) the country is not exempt from seismic disasters. A list compiled from the historical records mentions 3394 earthquakes for the 3693 years between 1767 B. C. and 1896 A. D.[20] The greatest catastrophe of this nature occurred in 1556 in the Wei Ho Valley when 800,000 people of Shensi, Shansi, and Honan are said to have lost their lives. Among the regions most subject to seismic disturbances particular interest attaches to the Kansu-Shensi area because of the geological nature of the terrain. This area is in the loess, the peculiar yellow-colored silt or loam that covers vast areas of northern China. Owing to the vertical cleavage of the loess the deeply eroded hills rise almost perpendicularly from the valleys, and a severe earthquake shock easily displaces this loose earth and causes it to slide down into the valleys in tremendous quantities. Seismic disturbances do not usually destroy sufficient foodstuffs to cause shortage, although the victims of such a cataclysm may suffer want for a few days until broken communications can be reëstablished. In the loess country, however, a severe quake may destroy both grain reserves and growing crops.

THE KANSU EARTHQUAKE OF 1920

In the great earthquake which occurred in eastern Kansu on December 16, 1920, there are several points of particular interest which are worthy of comment here. The severity of the distress following a quake is usually dependent upon the density of population and number of buildings in the affected district. For instance, the earthquake which took place in Vernyi, Turkestan, in 1911 resulted in but 400 deaths, although from a seismic point of view it was a severe shock; while more than 100,000 people are said to have perished in the Japan disaster of September 1, 1923, which demolished the populous cities of Yokohama and Tokyo. China is indeed a land of contrasts where almost every rule is broken. Here in Kansu it was the country population that suffered

[20] Wong Wen-Hao: L'influence sismogénique de certaines structures géologiques de la Chine, *Comptes Rendus Congrès Géol. Internatl. XIII*, Belgium, 1922, fasc. 2, Liége, 1925, pp. 1161–1197.

FIG. 39

FIG. 40

FIG. 39—In the Kansu earthquake mountains of loess slid into the valleys.
FIG. 40—Cave dwellings in the loess country.

the most. This is easily explainable. Scarcity of wood has forced the farmers to make their homes in caves which they excavate in the hillsides.[21] Very few of the cave dwellers in the affected district escaped, for the first shock occurred at 7 p. m., and, since it was winter time and dark, the people were all in their earthen retreats and were buried under many feet of loose earth before they realized what was taking place. The city of Kuyüan with a population of about 70,000 reported only 400 deaths, while 40,000 perished in the surrounding country districts.

Since this disaster occurred in the early part of the winter the crops had all been harvested, the threshing was done, and the supply of grain needed to support the family until the next harvest was stored in the cliff dwellings. It thus happened that the grain reserves in the area worst affected were practically all destroyed.

The change effected in the topography by this earthquake was very great. Landslides blocked the rivers, in many cases changing their courses. Some of the dams were as much as a mile thick and tens of feet in height; and, though every effort was made by the people and relief committees to open them before the high-water season, in some places it was impossible to do anything, and much distress was caused by floods.

THE YUNNAN EARTHQUAKE OF 1925

The earthquake which took place in Western Yunnan on March 16, 1925, did not present any unusual features. The greatest loss of life occurred in the urban districts. Fortunately the population was not dense, for one out of every eighteen was killed over an area of six counties. The destitute, who numbered nearly 100,000, were left without food, clothing, or shelter. Such a condition in China invariably means the starvation of a considerable number of people, and the Chinese are accustomed to regard such local distress as a famine. According to the accepted usage of the term in other countries, it is hardly correct to list a catastrophe such

[21] For a discussion of the type of habitation see M. L. Fuller and F. G. Clapp: Loess and Rock Dwellings of Shensi, China, *Geogr. Rev.*, Vol. 14, 1924, pp. 215–226.

as occurred at Talifu as a famine emergency. It must be remembered, however, that there are few other countries where an adjustment of the destitute population could not have been so effected as to prevent any appreciable number from dying for lack of food.

TYPHOONS

The China coast is not subject to the tidal waves, so-called, of seismic or volcanic origin; but the southeastern coast is frequently visited by severe wind storms or typhoons, and a phenomenon not greatly different from a tidal wave occurs where the sea walls are destroyed and the lands along the shores are flooded by sea water. The average number of typhoons is sixteen a year. These cyclonic storms gather in the Pacific Ocean near the island of Guam and take a northwesterly direction, rarely reaching as far north as Shanghai. The storm center moves forward at from 8 to 50 miles an hour, and the wind, which blows in a circle counterclockwise around the center, varies from 50 to 110 miles an hour in velocity.

The damage from typhoons is restricted to a narrow area along the coast; suffering is caused mainly by the destruction of property, and loss of life by falling buildings. Many animals are killed, but the crops are not affected excepting where the sea walls are destroyed and salt water invades the fields. The loss of foodstuffs from disasters of this sort is not sufficient to cause famine, although there is some loss of life from starvation after a severe visitation such as occurred at Swatow in the summer of 1922.

FIG. 41—The oft-quoted Chinese pacifism is a myth: an army on the march.

CHAPTER III

POLITICAL CAUSES OF FAMINE

China, although so often spoken of as a pacifist country, has seen as much if not more civil strife than any Western power. Mark Twain neither consulted history nor studied Chinese conditions when he remarked that "a disorderly Chinaman was a rare bird." He had probably heard something about the quietism which is the basis of Chinese philosophy. Or perhaps this was one of the rare bits of humor that made him so justly famous. Chinese pacifism is a beautiful ideal which has never, so far as the facts show, been taken down from its high theoretical plane and applied to the concrete requirements of daily existence. Chinese provinces have rebelled time and time again against the central authority. The histories are full of accounts of these numberless insurrections and the expeditions sent to quell them. China has carried out conquests as wide as those of any other great power, and the Hans even before the Christian era ruled a territory greater in extent than the contemporary Roman Empire—territory wrested by force from unwilling races. It will be said, of course, that the average Chinese does not like to fight and does not admire war. But what reasonable man does?

The Government and the Revolution of 1911

In the whole course of its dynastic history from the third century before Christ, when feudalism came to an end, to 1911, there was no change in the fundamental concepts of the government of monarchical China. This is the more remarkable in that throughout all these years the government was a government of men, not a government of laws. But Confucian political theory was so pervasive that it almost took on the form of a constitution, leading some writers to say that China's old system was a perfect example of a constitutional monarchy. Other writers sometimes refer to the base of China's monarchical government as theocratic; but this hardly seems to be warranted by the facts. True it is that the occupant of the throne was sometimes called the Son of Heaven, holding his commission from above; but not enough stress is placed on the elusive language with which the Chinese clothe their thought. Chinese emperors were never really thought of as divine appointees in the sense that they were responsible only to a Supreme Being. They were not even regarded as absolutists; nor did they ever claim to be. Most founders of new dynasties were content to claim kinship with past emperors, or with persons of noble birth, in order to justify their assumption of sovereign power.

It seems to the writer that the proper approach to the Chinese monarchical system is that taken by the Chinese themselves—that the people are the sea and the emperor a boat on the sea. If the sea became too stormy, then the boat capsized and that was the end of it. This more adequately expressed the Chinese idea than the explanation sometimes offered to excuse the frequent challenges to kingly power, namely, that the emperor's mandate from Heaven had been exhausted. Chinese government was not divine but personal, paternalistic; the people were the children of Heaven and the emperor was the father of the people, duly approved by his children and responsible to them.

In such an intensely paternalistic state, good government depended in a peculiar way on good men, and, if any king showed particular goodness and beneficence, his people gradually enveloped him in their speech and memorials with heavenly attributes, perhaps as the Son of Heaven. But this was merely a tribute to his rule and the regard in which he was held by his subjects; the people were specially favored by Heaven to have such a king father.

It follows that the overthrow of an old dynasty and the establishment of a new one involved troubles enough to affect production materially. Disorganization must have gone on many years before the close of the dynasty. That was the reason for its displacement, and misrule and oppression had to go some lengths in China before displacement could be effected. The Chinese are proverbially lacking in organization, as we understand it, and a reigning house long outlived the period of its beneficence and of its mandate before it was deposed. As a matter of fact, of the two ways in which a personal government can be overthrown—by aggression from without or by discord from within—changes in China have been brought about more often by alien elements. Discord would sometimes simmer for years until some outside force succeeded in stirring it into a political upheaval.

But the 1911 revolution, which saw the collapse of the Manchu house, was inspired and carried out from within. Even at the time of the Taiping Rebellion the throne had exhausted its mandate; but outside agencies in this case were employed, not to succeed it but to prop it up. It languished on, effete and enwrapt in a formalism which negatived its paternalistic functions, until the dawn of the twentieth century, when the Boxer Rebellion would probably have consigned it to oblivion but for the adroit turning of the tide of revolt in the direction of the foreigners. And it was the foreigner again that was responsible for the return to power of the dynasty. In 1911, after these two attempts at artificial respiration, it expired, leaving no head to take its place.

For three thousand years the Middle Kingdom had been governed like a family by a king father. In 1911 the people had the power suddenly thrust into their own hands, and it was their task to transplant the idea of sovereignty in themselves; in other words to personify the idea of the state. The task might have been easier if the leaders of the revolution had been possessed of some plan or organization. But they had only many paper plans culled from textbooks and no organization except those bred in secret societies. No genius appeared who could become a new "Father of the People" until the abstract idea of sovereignty had evolved into a force equal to that exercised through the throne. "Let there be men, and the government will flourish," said Confucius. "Without the men, government decays and ceases." The breakdown of government, as old China knew it, is now probably more complete than it has been for centuries.

There being no new outstanding leaders in the new republic, the old officials came into possession of the reins of government. A so-called republican administration was set up in Peking, but it endeavored to function according to the old monarchical plan of centralized authority at the capital, every provincial official of any importance being selected by a more or less self-appointed "president." This central authority has grown weaker and weaker until at present its mandates are practically without effect. In the meantime, the military leaders in the various provinces, realizing their power and subject to no restraining influence, have worked each for himself, rising and falling like the tide. Temporary combinations are effected for the purpose of eliminating any one who appears to be gaining the ascendency; but, when this is accomplished, the allies split up to fight among themselves until the time is ripe for another effort at military consolidation.

All men are equal; all claim the same privilege of preying on their fellows. The idea of responsibility to the state, in the absence of a monarch, is not yet envisaged; it hardly enters at all into the consideration of modern Chinese leaders, for the reason that the old spirit of family enrichment at the expense of other families is the paramount motive.

Destruction of Public Granary System

One of the first results of the overthrow of the Manchu régime—and a matter of vital importance in time of famine— was the abolition of the public granaries maintained in the provinces. The accumulation of a surplus of foodstuffs against times of need was a long-established policy of the government. Every year the farmers were required to turn over a portion of their grain crops to the authorities for storage in the public granaries, which were kept full. To prevent the stock from deteriorating with age as much old grain was sold each year as was received of new. By this system there was available in all walled cities throughout the interior a surplus of food which was distributed in times of want. While this did not prevent famines when the crops failed over wide areas, it greatly mitigated the suffering of the people, saved some lives, and was a means by which the population might be fed before relief from outside was available. In minor disasters these supplies were sufficient to meet the needs. This was the plan followed with conspicuous success by Joseph in Egypt.

It was said that the contents of the granaries were sold in 1912 in order to "defray the expenses of the revolution"; but the granaries have not been restocked by the republican government, and this most important system is now abandoned. Nowhere in China proper, but only in sparsely populated and distant Tibet, are public granaries now to be found.

Even before the revolution the effectiveness of the granary system began to fall off, owing to official corruption. The following passage from the *Peking Gazette* quoted in "Chinese Life in Town and Country," by H. Twitchell, shows the condition of affairs in 1897.

The censor Chang-chao-lan denounces the practice, prevalent among the magistrates, of speculating with the cereals stored in the public granaries, with the result that they become bankrupt and are unable to settle their accounts with the Government. The functionaries should constantly bear in mind that every walled city must reserve in its public granaries a quantity of cereals proportioned to its population, to be distributed in case of inundations, famine, war, or other disaster. They are authorised, however, to sell a certain portion of the old stock and replenish it with the fresh harvest. Instead of doing that, the censor accuses them of allowing the old grain to mould in the granaries and of selling the fresh for their own profit. It is easy to foresee what the result of such a course would be in

Fig. 42

Fig. 43

Fig. 42—The flood that swept Kalgan in 1924 could have been prevented if official action had been taken in time.

Fig. 43—The Shantung flood of the Yellow River, 1925, was due to official negligence.

time of need. We seriously exhort the divers viceroys and governors of our provinces to look into this matter and order the entire stock of cereals sold, the proceeds to be placed at interest. Furthermore, we order each magistrate to submit to us each year an exact account of the amounts so placed and of the contents of the public storehouses.[22]

REMISSION OF TAXES IN FAMINE YEARS

One of the first ameliorative measures adopted by effective governments in China in the past has been tax remission in the famine districts during the period of distress. This custom is followed in principle even now during these days of disorganization but not in a manner to afford the people material help. For, while the tax is remitted to the starving country population, new methods of obtaining revenue are devised by the military officials, methods that greatly increase prices and more than offset the benefits of the remitted tax. These new methods of securing an increased income range all the way from petty taxes on luxuries to a heavy levy on necessities—as, for instance, salt—and include such innovations as a re-registry fee for all land deeds at an exorbitant figure. Coupled with these more or less orderly processes of obtaining funds is the practice in times of emergency of a demand on Chambers of Commerce for huge "loans," the collection of taxes several years in advance, and the issue of millions of dollars in worthless paper notes forced on merchants at the point of the bayonet.

Were this revenue utilized for maintaining a decent and efficient administration, its collection would not so seriously affect the people, for the total sum is not great when compared with the receipts of other governments; but, unfortunately, the great bulk of it goes to the enrichment of unscrupulous officials.

Relief funds too have been misappropriated. After the disastrous floods of 1924 the government was importuned to undertake relief work. After some delay it was decided that a surtax should be imposed throughout the country

[22] H. Twitchell: Chinese Life in Town and Country, Adapted from the French of Émile Bard (Series: Our Asiatic Neighbors), New York, 1905, pp. 91–92.

on all railway tickets and telegrams to raise funds for famine purposes. It was called a famine-relief surtax and was collected for over a year. After a lapse of some months inquiries were made as to how the receipts were being utilized, but up to the present time no statement has ever been made of the amount collected. In only one or two districts, where the funds were not remitted to Peking but were spent by the local authorities, were the proceeds of this surtax known to have been expended for famine relief. The surtax was first imposed for a period of six months. At the end of that time it was extended for the avowed purpose of raising funds for the support of the government universities in Peking, but it was still called a famine-relief surtax. It is not even possible to state whether or not the funds collected were used for the universities: the Famine Commission has been unable to find any published reports.

Famine Prevention Neglected

Grievous as is the failure of the government to provide succor for the population in time of famine, its most serious shortcoming is its neglect of necessary prevention work. It is this neglect that has caused such an increase in the number and severity of famines in late years.

A period of poor government is always marked by serious floods. As has been explained before, most of China's rivers are artificially controlled by an extensive and intricate system of diking. These dikes, built centuries ago, must be constantly maintained and occasionally heightened. Changes in the course of the rivers between the dikes require the construction of special works to avert the danger of breaches during the high-water season, and an organization must be supported to patrol the rivers and to plan and execute the needed repairs. Constant disintegration of government results in smaller and smaller appropriations for this needed work. The Chinese social system, stressing the family unit, has failed to develop a community spirit or to encourage coöperation of individuals outside the family, among families, villages, or districts.

In the few places where flood-prevention organizations exist, they are as devoid of public spirit as are the government authorities, being in fact semi-official in character. There is a typical example of the workings of such organizations in the Fifth Annual Report of the Board of Conservancy Works of Kwangtung, a board which is to a large extent divorced from Chinese official influence. The opposition, which has so far been successful, to a permanent scheme of dike improvement near Canton emanates from the local dike committees, who found their positions jeopardized by the Board's activities. These committees, who collect yearly from the farmers large sums of money supposed to be used for the maintenance of the dikes, deemed it contrary to their interests that a permanent scheme of improvement should be provided and financed by others than themselves— in this case by the Board.

A striking example of a disaster due to official negligence is the Yellow River flood of 1925 in western Shantung. Under the old régime the conservancy of the Yellow River along its whole course was unified under the control of one man who reported directly to the Emperor. The annual appropriation for the upkeep of the river dikes was about three million dollars. Now this unified control is no longer continued, and each provincial governor is charged with the maintenance of the river within his territory. These governors, however, apply the public funds to the support of military establishments or to the waging of war on neighboring satraps. Appropriations for river conservancy grow smaller and smaller. The break in the main south dike occurred simply from lack of proper upkeep, for only a few tens of thousands of dollars can have been spent in 1924; and most of this must have gone for organization expenses, not for works.

To the losses from failure to maintain the existing conservancy works must be added the much greater loss from failure to undertake new works. Most of the schemes proposed by modern engineers are economically sound, and the new revenue which would result from them would soon

Fig. 44

Fig. 45

Fig. 44—Where the water of the old Shensi Irrigation Scheme divided.
Fig. 45—The present main canal of the Shensi Irrigation Scheme. Built 2000 years ago.

cover the initial cost. Foreign nations, particularly the United States, have funds to loan for such productive enterprises. But there is no stable government in China, and hence no security. The last loan of any importance for work of this kind to come from America was for the improvement

Fig. 46—There is always migration of people during famine. These are refugees in Hunan.

of the Grand Canal. A contract was signed with the Central Government. American engineers were employed to make a comprehensive survey of a scheme to prevent floods and improve transportation, and more than a million dollars was loaned by the American group. Not only have present conditions prevented consummation of the project, but the Government has not even paid the interest on the sum already advanced.

In the same way the development of China's transportation system, which would do much to prevent and relieve famines, is hindered solely by the unsatisfactory political condition of the country. Railway lines already in operation are rapidly going to ruin, for their revenue is appropriated by the military chieftains and no provision is made for upkeep. In times of serious conflicts, which occur now practically every year, the entire line is commandeered and moves no traffic except troops and supplies. This state of things may continue for weeks or months, and then the badly damaged rolling stock will again be put at the service of the public to provide revenue for the successful military leader. In some cases, where there are several military holders of

FIG. 47—What chance for normal traffic when the stations are blocked with troop trains?

a line, the revenues are divided, each general taking the receipts of the area under his direct control.

In such circumstances it is not surprising that China has not paid even the interest on some of her railway loans, and that the amortization of others is delayed. No adequate extension of the railways can be expected while such conditions last. Improvement of rivers for navigation purposes, building of roads, and repair and extension of canals are all in the same category, and all await establishment of a stable government.

BANDITRY

Unsettled conditions in China always increase banditry, and bandits are not only nonproducers but actual destroyers of property. In areas subject to their raids the initiative of the people is tremendously crippled. Many rich districts have been so overrun that the population has been forced to leave the land and take to the hills, where they can more easily protect themselves, or to seek new homes where security can be enjoyed.

Most of the bandits in China at present are the defeated troops of the various military leaders. One day they will be so-called government forces; the next, if overpowered by some rival force, they will take to the hills, carrying their arms and what ammunition they can scrape together with them, thereafter to eke out an existence by carefully planned raids on the more fortunate dwellers on the plains. Not only do these marauding bands carry off everything of any intrinsic value, but they ofttimes burn the villages and towns, especially if the value of their loot is not considered to represent the true wealth of their victims. It is also customary to capture prominent citizens or their families and hold them for ransom.

It is an interesting commentary on the people and on the times to note that, when bandits are successful in capturing some citizen of such importance as to give them a bargaining power with the government authorities, they invariably ask, not to be paid a large sum of money, but to be enrolled in the army of the faction that chances to be in power at the time. This would indicate that what they are chiefly concerned about is simply the assurance of sufficient food. They are not necessarily vicious but rather desperate people who, because of the political turmoil, have lost their means of support. They may have been enrolled in a distant province and, when they find their military chief defeated and their organization shattered, have no means of getting back to their homes, and the new régime is naturally unwilling to make a place for them. Banditry is almost their only recourse. Moreover, the oppressed farmers are occasionally reduced to banditry as the only means of insuring a bare subsistence, and thousands of the highwaymen in China at present would be self-respecting citizens in normal times. They have been driven to the hills and lawlessness by hunger and continued extortion; having been preyed upon almost to death, they have chosen to reverse the rôle mainly at the expense of other unfortunates who have not their courage and will to live.

EXCESS TROOPS

As far as the civilian population is concerned the soldiery are not much better than the bandits. They live off the

FIG. 48—A fortified point used as a refuge against bandits in the hill country of Shensi.

country in which they are billeted. The only difference is that they belong, technically, to the government forces, and the supplies which they need are commandeered according to a more regular procedure. In the last analysis the hardworking peasant population foots the bill, whether at the point of a bandit's gun or at the courteous behest of a military satrap.

With conditions as they now are in China, the tremendous army maintained by the various provinces is probably drawn from surplus labor, and loss in production is not so great as would at first appear. However, other economic loss is sustained from this cause. According to the China Year Book, there were approximately 1,404,000 men in the various armies in 1924. Since that time there has been strenuous recruiting in many of the provinces, and, if the bandits also are included, it is probably no exaggeration to say that there are now no less than two million men under arms. It is estimated that the cost of maintaining a soldier is about $200 a year. But the estimate of the living standard given in a former chapter allows the average family of five members only $150, and this, according to available statistics, is more than is actually spent. Assuming that the proportion of the $150 consumed by an adult is about $40, it costs five times as much to keep a man in the army as it does at home; and the loss to the country, even if we place the number of troops at the conservative figure of 1,500,000 and assume that all the men are normally unproductive, would reach $240,000,000 annually. This does not include the loss of revenue on the railways from free transportation of men and supplies. Neither does it include the immense sums spent for ammunition, artillery, airplanes, and other auxiliary equipment.

But while the soldiers are recruited from surplus labor, the animals used for the transport of ammunition and supplies, to draw the guns, and to serve as mounts for the officers and cavalry are taken from production, for there is no surplus of domestic animals corresponding to the surplus of population. This item entails a loss in addition to the cost of feeding the animals, depending upon the season when they are impressed; for it is not the custom to maintain ammunition and supply trains constantly but to commandeer carts when needed. If a campaign begins in the plowing season, it causes greater hardship to the people than in the slack of the year. But even then it is customary to work the animals either for grinding, to pump water for irrigation, or for cartage.

One of the contributory causes of the famine in 1925 in central China was the civil strife between Kweichow and Szechwan. The Kweichow troops invaded southern Szechwan and after some fighting were driven out. When they left they took with them all available beasts of burden, loaded with grain. The Szechwan troops who replaced them brought very little in the way of supplies and forthwith appropriated the remainder of the food reserves of the district—leaving the population, who had no interest in either side, to starve.

Heavy Taxation by Unscrupulous Officials

There is no doubt that this great drain on the resources of the country tends to increase the frequency and severity of famine distress. The heavy taxes imposed by the militarists to keep up their establishments tend to increase prices, and this in turn makes living more difficult for the poorer classes, although the taxes may be collected from their more fortunate brethren.

Many of the methods employed by military leaders to collect revenues are of a nature to upset the economic equilibrium and restrict trade and, in some instances, to affect vitally the well-being of the individual. In the first category may be named the appropriation of the revenues of the railways, which has already been mentioned. In this class may be counted also the likin, or transit taxes, imposed at frequent intervals along the main routes of commerce and reaching such proportions as to stifle trade. This is one of the reasons that makes German porcelain cheaper than Kiangsi porcelain in Peking, in spite of its much higher production cost. The German product is imported through Tientsin and is liable to only two regular taxes, the import duty and the octroi tax on entering Peking; whereas porcelain from Kiangsi Province, in traveling a distance of only eight or nine hundred miles through interior China, may be subject to as many as sixty different imposts en route, depending in both number and amount almost solely on the whim of the war lords through whose areas the product has to pass.

It is customary to tax rice exported from some provinces on the plea of a poor harvest and the need for retaining all available supplies for local use. But actually this is done many times simply as a means for increasing the revenue of the local chieftain. The effect is to make the movement of grain difficult and to prevent needy provinces from re-

ceiving the surplus of neighboring districts except at exorbitant prices.   Such a condition existed in the provinces of
central China in 1925, and the price of rice rose to unprec-
edented heights in many centers.   This was another of the
contributing causes of the famine distress in this region.

THE OPIUM TRAFFIC

A still greater evil perpetrated for similar purposes is the
wholesale engagement of officials in the growth, transportation, and sale of opium.   In many provinces the greatest
source of income is from opium.   In order to "prevent"
the growing of the poppy from which opium is derived it
is the custom to impose an opium tax on the farmers.   Every
acre of poppy is taxed with the declared purpose of making
it difficult for the farmers to raise this crop.   However, the
tax is not imposed on the acreage actually under cultivation
for poppy raising but on the land known to be suitable for
this purpose.   The tax is so high that the farmer is unable
to raise any other crop but opium, while the revenue from
this product is sufficient not only to pay the tax but also
to leave a handsome profit.   Naturally the farmer raises
the poppy, and the "governor" suavely protests that he
is doing his best to curb the evil.   The transportation of
opium from one province to another and its sale are also
often so arranged as to leave a profit in the hands of the
officials.   License fees for opium dens and houses of ill-
repute serve to swell the total emoluments from this source.

A glaring example of official rapacity and oppression
occurred in Fukien Province a few years ago.   Hearing that
some opium suppression mission was on its way to his area,
a local chieftain hurriedly called in the collection of the
opium tax two years in advance and then ordered the destruction of the crops.

It is not only the injurious effect of the opium habit—
a remote cause of famine in itself—that most seriously concerns us but also the growth of the poppy on rich grain
lands, which very materially decreases the food supply of

FIG. 49

FIG. 50

FIG. 49—Dry rice fields; the crop a total failure. Tax remittance and other government aid were formerly given in time of famine.

FIG. 50—Opium poppies on grain land. Good government could prevent opium growing.

the country. This was a third contributing cause of the famine in central China in 1925.

Government Action Needed to Relieve Overcrowding

From Chinese origins the general trend of migration of the people seems to have been in a southerly rather than a northerly direction. According to archeological authority the Chinese who first achieved political and cultural solidarity resided along the middle reaches of the Yellow River.[23] With the passage of time they made their way down the valley and turned southward until the southern part of China was settled, while from the southern coast there was eventually a movement overseas. Rich and fertile lands in Mongolia and Manchuria have been left aside and even now are sparsely populated. Whatever the reasons in the past there would seem little excuse for such neglect under present conditions of overpopulation. Among the contributing causes must be included the failure of the government to protect the colonizers against the inroads of the wild Mongolian tribes, as well as from the Chinese bandits with which the sparsely populated districts in the North are cursed.

The government has failed to provide means forcibly to move the excess of population from overcrowded regions in normal times and give them sufficient support and protection so that they might get a foothold in the new country; or even in times of famine to utilize the relief funds in directing and assisting the starving wanderers to a place where they could eventually support themselves.

But, while no adequate government-organized and supported effort has been made to colonize the North and Northwest, there is in progress a slow but steady movement of the population of the northern provinces of China proper in that direction. However, it is not fast enough to have any appreciable effect on the congestion of the plains, for the places of the few who move out are soon filled. It would take a comprehensive and well arranged plan to achieve

[23] See for instance C. W. Bishop: The Geographical Factor in the Development of Chinese Civilization. *Geogr. Rev.*, Vol. 12, 1922, pp. 19-41.

success. Such a scheme could be carried out only by the government, for the people would move only under real pressure, and the officials up to the present time have not had the authority nor the resources nor the desire to bring it to fruition.

It is interesting to note that a cause of the lack of initiative which might induce the residents of the overcrowded, famine-threatened northern provinces to seek better opportunities may be traceable to the effects on the race of former oft-repeated starvation conditions. Professor Ellsworth Huntington in his recent book "The Character of Races," in comparing the home-loving, conservative, slow-to-act natives of the northern provinces of China to the radical, progressive, adventurous southerners, ascribes the difference to the selective effect of famines on successive generations. These northern families, he thinks, have developed habits of thrift and economy until the acquisitive instinct has become second nature, for the wasteful and extravagant have long since been eliminated during the many years of want. These characteristics are the natural counterpart of conservatism, a desire to keep at all costs what has been acquired, and they tend to make abhorrent the thought of leaving home and giving up a plot of land, however meager and inadequate to support a growing family.

FIG. 51—Many dikes form natural roadways suitable for motor traffic

CHAPTER IV

SOCIAL CAUSES OF FAMINE

In the last analysis the principal cause of most famines in China, which it must be remembered is an agricultural country, is a density of population greater than the land is able to support. It may be well to examine this vexed question of population in some detail.

Chinese Population Statistics

As with most fundamental information in China, all arguments based on population must remain unsupported by exact figures. To quote Mr. H. B. Elliston of the Chinese Government Bureau of Economic Information:

Were it not for the fact that there is a lack of statistical data on both production and population in China, it might be possible to assess this problem of population in more definitive terms. But as Dr. Arthur Smith in reply to a newspaper request for the "bottom facts" of a Chinese situation once said, there is no bottom in China, and no facts. One can only speak from an experience of the country which, no matter how long the residence or how observant the mind, can at the best be merely a cursory survey. Such is the magnitude of China.

There is no official census of persons, and unofficial estimates of China's population vary within wide limits. The Manchus issued population statistics in 1651, but these were on the basis of tax-paying households, not individuals. According to these figures there were 10,633,326 households in China at that time. In 1734, according to Professor E. H. Parker's "China: Past and Present," there were 26,500,000 households in all China. If we allow five souls to a household,

84

this would give us a total population of 130,000,000. Two years after, in 1736, the great Ch'ien Lung came to the throne, ruling for sixty years, expanding and consolidating the Manchu régime. He devised a more intelligent system than that based on tax-paying households. From 1741 to 1851 this system gave a year-by-year tabulation of population, showing a steadily mounting return of souls, beginning with 143,411,559 and ending with the maximum of 432,164,047.[24] Professor Parker goes on to say that the population of China cannot at any time have much exceeded 100,000,000 until the beginning of the eighteenth century. By the year 1762 it had over-topped 200,000,000, doubling itself during the next century. This is a slower rate of increase than the present average for the world. G. H. Knibbs, in his "Mathematical Theory of Population," published by the Australian Government, gives 1,649,000,000, with a rate of increase of 1.159— that is, doubling in 60.15 years. Even if the Manchus followed the statistical method known to the West, which may be doubted, they did not maintain it; nor has the Republic taken the trouble to obtain any accurate census of the Chinese people. The last purely Chinese census was undertaken in 1910 and gives 327,079,000. Two estimates are commonly quoted by yearbooks and directories—one, an estimate by the foreign-supervised Maritime Customs, and the other by the Post Office. For 1924 these figures were: Post Office estimate, 436,094,953; Maritime Customs estimate, 444,653,-000. It is even difficult to compare them, as they do not embrace all the territory claimed to be under Chinese suzerainty.

In a recent discussion of China's population problem Professor Roxby of the University of Liverpool compares the Post Office census of 1920 with the China Continuation Committee's survey of 1917–1918.[25] The respective figures are 427,679,000, 440,925,000. In both instances the population is exclusive of Inner and Outer Mongolia and Sinkiang

[24] E. H. Parker: China: Past and Present, London, 1903, p. 27.

[25] P. M. Roxby: The Distribution of Population in China: Economic and Political Significance, *Geogr. Rev.*, Vol. 15, 1925, pp. 1–24. The China Continuation Committee published their results in a volume entitled "The Christian Occupation of China," Shanghai, 1922. Figs. 10, 11, 12, 13, and 14 are from this volume.

and Tibet with Kokonor but is inclusive of Manchuria. The compilers of the China Continuation Committee were inclined to consider their estimate as too high.

POPULATION FIGURE ARBITRARY

It will readily be seen from the above data that the writer on China has to choose from many conflicting estimates and in the end has to fall back on a more or less arbitrary figure. What shall that figure be? Judging from the Manchu estimates up to the middle of the last century and bearing in mind the rate of progression of Chinese population, it would seem that the Maritime Customs and Post Office are too conservative. But several factors have operated in the last seventy years against the natural increase. The great Taiping Rebellion (1856–1860) is said to have more than decimated the population. Then there were the terrible famine in northern China of 1877—1878, the Mohammedan Rebellion in western China in 1861-1862, and other retarding influences. These factors, coupled with the natural facility of the Chinese for talking in round numbers, have caused many authorities, the most notable being the late W. W. Rockhill, former United States Minister to China, to depreciate the usual estimate of China's population as 400,000,000.[26] The writer, however, is inclined to consider that figure as, if anything, below the actual, having seen many evidences of the remarkable recuperative power of the Chinese and its effect in the multiplication of the species. Truly, the people in the interior of China live in layers, fitted into the most miserable shacks it has been the writer's misfortune to see.

Fifty years ago the islands that dot the West Lake in the province of Chihli supported very few people, according to old records and the statements of old residents. Today they are teeming with life. On one island, half a square mile in area, Ch'uantou, the writer was informed by a Salva-

[26] W. W. Rockhill: Inquiry into the Population of China, *Smithsonian Misc. Colls.*, Vol. 47, 1904, pp. 303–321, and *idem:* The 1910 Census of the Population of China, *Bull. Amer. Geogr. Soc.*, Vol. 44, 1912, pp. 668–673.

tion Army resident missionary that there were over seven hundred families. This is still the usual way in China of computing population; and at the number of persons to a family we have previously allowed, this would mean 4000 souls, or 8000 to the square mile! In this particular case there was no economic reason for the congestion of population. The people all eked out a sparse subsistence from the fish in the lake, buying their grain mostly in exchange for lake products and matting made from lakeside reeds. Here is a vivid illustration of Edwin Markham's "twin brother to the ox."

Thus the problem, in so far as it can be dealt with statistically. Personal observation shows that the fecundity of the Chinese is without parallel. It was vividly brought to the notice of a friend of the writer, newly-arrived in the Orient. He employed six servants in his modest establishment at a total monthly cost in actual wages (which it must be allowed is not the only reckoning in this land of "squeeze") of about forty dollars, United States currency. One day he asked his "boy" if he was married. "Yes," he replied, "and I have six children." Amazed that such a young man should have a family of six and more amazed that he could support them on his meager wages, my friend continued his inquiries and found that no fewer than thirty-two persons were being supported by him through his six servants.

High Birth Rate in China

In spite of the tremendously high death rate, particularly of infants, due to lack of modern medical knowledge, in spite of the depopulating effect of terrible famines, and in spite of the immense loss of life caused by civil wars we find today a denser population on the plains than ever before; and since there has been no appreciable influx from other countries we must ascribe the present conditions to the excessively high birth rate.

Reasons are not far to seek. In the first place, a study of the comparative birth rate of various classes in other coun-

tries shows that it is the uneducated, laboring population
that is the most prolific. Since the professional classes are
but an infinitesimal part of the total population, this fact
alone would have a large bearing on the situation. But it
is necessary to look deeper for the cause of the present conditions in the Orient, for even the casual foreign observer who
resides in China is impressed with the large families of those
who occupy the highest places both in official and intellectual
circles. Leaders of modern Chinese thought who have spent
years in the West and who have been educated in foreign
universities return to their homeland to raise families limited
in size only by the physical fitness of the parents. So it
is very evident that there is some compelling force making
for reproduction—a force superior to the dire effects of
overpopulation and the pitiful economic poverty of the great
masses.

Effect of Ancestor Worship on the Birth Rate

This force is the necessity of providing sufficient male
children so that, in spite of the ravages of disease, accident,
wars, pestilence, or famine, at least one will survive to carry
on the family name and perform the necessary duties required
by ancestor worship—the universal religion of the country.
No one not intimately acquainted with China realizes how
deeply rooted in the individual Chinese is the Confucian
doctrine of worshiping those who have gone before. An
elaborate ritual has grown up through the ages around this
practice; and it is only the male descendants who are qualified
to perform the necessary rites. One would gather from some
writers that China is a land without spirituality and without
an effective religion. Nothing could be further from the
truth. In spite of the fact that there are in China more
than 8000 foreign missionaries, Catholic and Protestant,
and that many tens of millions of dollars are expended annually in mission work, Christianity has had little effect in
changing the outlook of the Chinese upon life and its origin.
Chinese views are grounded in a vast imaginative cosmogony,

FIG. 52

FIG. 53

FIG. 54

FIG. 52—Sometimes the flood waters contain fish and help eke out the food supply.

FIG. 53—Countryside in the flooded area in Chihli months after the high-water season, covered by a vast sheet of ice.

FIG. 54—Fishing through the ice in a flooded region in northern China.

distinctly Oriental and steeped in mysticism. China's aversion to Christianity is the expression not of a lack of religion but of a natural repugnance to another code diametrically opposed to its own. A concrete example of the hold which ancestor worship has on the people is the case of the cathedral congregation of a large mission in central China who importuned the bishop to grant permission for the erection of ancestral tablets in the church. This was accorded, and many tablets are now installed, but the spirit which prompted their erection was far deeper than the wish merely to preserve the memory of some loved one, which is the guiding motive in the West.

The failure to reach the Chinese on the spiritual side has resulted in the diversion of many mission enterprises to industrial, educational, and hospital work: and it has been difficult for the masses of the people with their poverty, love of education, and need for medical attention, to decline this assistance. But the acceptance of such help should not be regarded as an indication that the traditional hostility to foreign beliefs has been relaxed.

Old-Age Insurance

Another cogent reason for the wish to have large families is to provide support for the parents' declining years. This is the old-age insurance policy of the Chinese. In the poorer classes especially many children are desired, particularly males, in order that at least one or two of them may live to maturity and care for their parents when the latter are no longer able to make a living. The feeling of obligation of a child toward its parents is so much a part of the character of the individual Chinese that it is only in exceptional cases that a son fails to put first the interests of his father and mother and even of his older brother. There are few opportunities for saving, especially in the villages; and this procedure furnishes the best possible assurance for declining years. Its weakness lies in the fact that probably a greater sum is expended in rearing a large family than is returned to the parents

in their old age. Many children are supported who die before
productive years; and the effort to raise sons results in at
least an equal number of daughters, who are regarded as a
total loss.

When a married pair have no children of their own it is
customary for them to adopt or purchase male infants, a
practice followed not only by the well-to-do but also by the
poorer classes. Widows do not often remarry in China,
and, if left childless, even they will undertake the support
of an adopted son as a means of insurance.

Early Marriage and Concubinage

A custom which results in large families is early marriage.
It is usual in China for marriages to be arranged by the parents of the bride and groom, often while they are still infants.
Since they have no part in the selection of their mates, there
is no reason why they should wait until maturity before they
marry. Sometimes the contracting parties are scarcely more
than children, but usually, especially among the poorer classes,
the wedding does not occur until the groom is in a position to
support his wife. As is the case with so many other subjects
in China, there are no accurate marriage statistics, but general
opinion agrees that the marrying age is less there than in
occidental countries.

The practice of taking secondary wives undoubtedly has
the effect of increasing the birth rate to the extent that it
provides husbands for girls who might not otherwise marry.
This factor is probably not an important one in China, however, for the population statistics of the Famine Commission's rural survey show that there is an excess of males
under the age of fifty. There is no evidence to show that
China differs from other countries where female births
exceed the males, but it is undoubtedly true that female
infants do not get the careful attention in China accorded
to male, and there is probably a much heavier mortality
among women in the first years of early marriage than there
is in the West. The increase in birth rate due to the custom

of concubinage is probably offset by the decrease which follows from the fact that widows do not remarry as in the West.

Frugality of the Chinese

The Chinese are justly recognized to be a frugal people. The foreigner, and particularly the American, is tremendously impressed with the extremely efficient utilization of the material necessities which reach the hands of the people. The reason why the great natural resources of the country are not being better exploited is another matter. But with a given amount of material for the needs of food, clothing, and shelter, surely no other people can compare with the Chinese in the use they can get out of it. Take, for instance, shoes, which are made by the women of the household. A good pair of soles is purchased of a size to fit the largest pair of feet in the family, usually the father's. Cloth tops for them are then made from old cast-off garments. When the soles wear out around the edges they are cut down and used for making a new pair of shoes for the next largest pair of feet, and so on until the soles are entirely worn out or until they have been cut down to fit the baby. Then what is left of them is exchanged with the ragpicker for matches.

The Standard Oil Company sells kerosene oil in five-gallon tins. When they are empty they go to the tinsmith and are converted into dustpans and other useful household articles. Tin cans and even cigarette packages may be found at the fairs, disguised as toys. Absolutely nothing is wasted. The writer can recall having seen a rickshaw man wearing an abbreviated lady's jacket of the sort popular in New York in the early nineties and a cast-off "stove-pipe" hat, not in too bad condition—surely a ludicrous sight. But his appearance excited no comment from the passers-by. The coat was still warm and serviceable; and the hat, although not ideally suited to the wearer's use, was certainly better than none at all.

There is no doubt that too frugal habits and too niggardly a view of life are deterrent to progress. It is not so much that they foster "penny wise and pound foolish" practices, but they sap the initiative of the people. In their concentration on conserving the resources within their grasp, they ofttimes lose sight of the opportunity to increase their assets. There are many reasons why China is so poverty-

FIG. 55—One of the most wasteful ceremonies is funerals. (Photograph by Hartung.)

stricken despite her potential wealth, but not the least among them is the penurious outlook on life which prevents the individual from viewing the problems of his family and his country in the light of the tremendous possibilities of the future instead of the discouraging limitations of the present.

WASTE DUE TO CEREMONIES AND FEASTS

But this habit of economy is cast aside at frequent intervals, and a perfect orgy of wastefulness is indulged in for a brief season. The occasion for such lapses is found in the practice of celebrating some ceremony, most often a funeral, a birthday, a wedding, or some other event which vitally affects the family. The amount of money devoted to such purposes is quite likely out of all proportion to the income of the family. A birthday celebration, for instance, may start in the morning, last all day, and extend far into the night; theatricals are provided and a huge feast at a cost of hundreds and often thousands of dollars. Such entertainments, especially funerals, involve the burning of much paraphernalia— "money" made of tinfoil, imitation automobiles, sedan chairs, paper concubines and horses, and other articles which may be an assistance or a pleasure to the dead man when he arrives at his celestial home. Again, the Chinese being intensely superstitious may waste the savings of years in an orgy or feast on the occasion of an impending crack of doom, foretold from time to time as about to happen on a certain date.

One of the worst features of the practice of holding such elaborate ceremonies is the tendency to contract debt thereby. It is the families so handicapped that are the first to go under on the advent of disaster, for not only are their savings gone but even their credit is destroyed.

It is not alone the rich who indulge in these wasteful practices, but people of all classes; and the sums spent by the poor, while comparatively smaller, cause the greater distress. Vast amounts are frittered away every year in America, but the effect is not to impoverish the people to anything like the extent that a smaller waste produces in China. The proportion of income devoted to such uses in China will probably reach a much higher figure than abroad, notwithstanding the great difference in the standard of living, and this is the factor that counts.

The frequent feasts given in conjunction with official functions also add to the unnecessary depletion of the nation's food supply. These feasts are composed of numerous dishes, any one of which should be sufficient for an adequate meal for the average family. Occasionally as many as a hundred courses are served. The requirements for even a modest feast offered to a company of ten or at most twelve persons include: four cold dishes, six hot dishes, four "big" courses, two kinds of dessert, four varieties of fruit, four varieties of preserves, four kinds of dry nuts or nut candy. Rice of course, is indispensable; so is steamed bread.

During the various festivals and at civil ceremonies when friends get together and make merry, as many as fifty to a hundred feasts may be given at one place at the same time. The Chinese say that this social usage is so strong that for the leading members of a community to discontinue the practice of feast giving would be as hard as the elimination of rice from their diet.

A minor source of waste, mentioned by the writer simply because it has been impressed upon him in his relief work, is the great number of dogs—in the rural districts one or more to each household. Obviously they are intended as a protection against robbers and as scavengers, but these ends could be served with but a small part of the present numbers. If kept simply as pets, they are indeed an expensive luxury; for in the course of a year they consume an appreciable quantity of food, though by this it should not be inferred that they are well fed. Probably a leaner, fiercer, more pitifully neglected collection of dogs is not to be found anywhere in the world. Their condition serves to show how little surplus there is in a Chinese village for non-essentials; surely the maintenance of non-productive animals is a drain on the community that is particularly felt in the lean years.

Waste Due to Overeating

There is a general feeling among intelligent Chinese that a tremendous waste occurs each year from overeating. While people in one district are on the verge of starvation from poor crops, the residents of other districts where the harvest has been bountiful are eating more food than they need or can possibly digest. It is common opinion that the food consumption of the farming people is determined by the quantity of grain possessed by the family against the next harvest. Mr. Y. S. Djang, who is the foremost Chinese famine-relief administrator of the modern type, after an inquiry into this subject said:

In districts where the crops are reliable and abundant the rural population consumes more food than even their arduous labor requires. For instance, in eastern Chekiang, in the rice fields of Shaohsing, the farmers eat as much as three bowls of rice three times daily. Each bowl is in reality two bowls, for the content of one is placed on the top of that of another, and they count this "double strength" quantity as one. Supposing that each bowl contains one catty, the total which each individual eats every day is nine catties, or twelve pounds. In its dry state, this amount of rice weighs four pounds. Half of this quantity would certainly suffice even for an adult doing hard manual work.

The food consumed is only partially utilized when ejected from the human system, and the high fertilizing value of the human manure cast off by these people is well recognized. To induce the patronage of public latrines, the farmers build and maintain fairly elaborate outhouses in the country, providing toilet necessities.

In this particular section of eastern Chekiang mentioned above, the people consume all their soil will produce. Even in the best years when the crops are especially plentiful, I learned from the farmers that they never sell their produce in any quantity to outside buyers.

WASTE OF TIME

It is perhaps strange that the remarkable frugality in expenditure of the material things of life does not extend also to a saving of that greatest of all resources, time. Surely there are few places in the world where time means less to people than in China. The slogan of the West, "Time is money," not only strikes no responsive chord in the breast of the average Chinese but offends, in a sense, his idea of the dignity befitting a man of intelligence. The writer is of the opinion that there is a natural reason for this phenomenon, as there is for many of the other characteristics of the people. This reason, however, can scarcely be ascribed to climate. The climate in northern China, particularly—and it is here that the people are especially slow—is most invigorating. Neither can it be ascribed to laziness; for the Chinese, given a task, are exceptionally diligent, and the amount of work which an individual is capable of accomplishing, if put to it, is truly amazing.

The author believes that this attitude is the direct result of the overcrowding on the land. For every piece of work there are several workers. This situation applied to laborers who work for a wage undoubtedly tends to increase efficiency, but most of the labor in China is on the land; and for a given plot of ground belonging to or farmed by a family there are usually more workers than are needed. Moreover, the Chinese have so niched themselves into their places in the social and economic scale that they refuse to perform tasks, even minor tasks, that lie outside their daily round. Even if a minor job is accessory to and fits in with his own, a worker will shrug his shoulders and utter the Chinese equivalent to the widely known version in pidgin English, "No b'long my pidgin." This is the Oriental expression for the principle of one man, one job—the principle well known to Western trade unionism; and in China there is no doubt that, in conjunction with a certain amount of "soldiering on the job," it helps the maximum number to maintain employment.

And centuries of this condition have had their effect in slowing up the individual. There is a singular contrast in the atmosphere of a Japanese and a Chinese village. Japan has an air of bustle entirely lacking in China. Not only the men but also the women are constantly engaged in some useful occupation which serves to increase their income. The shopkeeper does not sit idly waiting for the next customer; and the women of the household, if not employed about their housekeeping duties, are engaged in some industry that adds to the family funds. In China the tremendous labor wastage keeps down production to a point where it has an important effect even on the number and severity of famines. Not only does it decrease the possible supply of foodstuffs, but it diminishes the creation of products which might be exchanged in other countries for food.

This waste of time was forced upon the writer's attention as he was making a trip through the part of interior China devastated by the Mohammedan Rebellion. Many of the villages over a wide area are totally ruined, and in others a large proportion of the houses are wrecked and only some few of them have been repaired, at least sufficiently to afford shelter. The writer was astonished to find that this destruction was wrought sixty-five years ago. In all this time the countryside has not been restored, and the blackened

ruins yet stand as they were left two generations ago. To
be sure, many of the former inhabitants were massacred;
but some were left, and others have since filled their places;
and all have made their homes amid the ruins with never
a thought of cleaning up and rebuilding the old abodes in
spite of the weeks and months of leisure during the winter
season. Contrast this condition with the rebuilding of the
devastated regions in the southern United States after
the Civil War, which took place simultaneously with the
Mohammedan Rebellion in China; or compare it with the
rehabilitation of the much more completely destroyed sections of Europe since the close of the World War in 1918,
and some idea of the backwardness of the people of interior
China may be envisaged.

Foot Binding

Another great form of labor wastage is to be found in the
custom of foot binding. Although some progress has been
made in eradicating this self-inflicted crippling of the female
population, it is only in a few places that any proportion of
the women are free from this curse. In the interior the writer
has traveled for days without seeing a single woman or girl
with normal feet. Many of the women labor in the fields in
spite of their infirmity, and it is surprising that they are
able to do so at all; but the amount of work which even the
most active can accomplish is comparatively small especially
in occupations which require walking or standing.

Land Used for Graves and Home Burial

A social custom having a direct bearing on the production
of food is that of setting apart immense areas for burial of
the dead. The most thickly populated regions where the
land is good and where it is most needed for agriculture are,
unfortunately, just the districts where graves are most
numerous. In many cases the mounds reach an enormous
size. The well-to-do often surround the family graves with
trees which prevents the use of the land for crop-growing

FIG. 56

FIG. 57

FIG. 58

FIG. 56—The well-to-do surround the family graves with trees, taking land almost permanently out of production.

FIG. 57—Some grave mounds reach an enormous size.

FIG. 58—Miles of grave mounds covering good grain land.

for many years, perhaps permanently. Graves made in open fields are more apt to be plowed up after a few generations when the elements have done their work of erosion and the outlines of the mounds have been lost.

There are no dependable statistics from which an exact estimate of the area of burial grounds can be made. It is probably no exaggeration to say, however, that not less than five per cent of the cultivable land in the densely populated provinces is at present devoted to this purpose.

At the overthrow of every dynasty there has been a tendency to plow up the old graves. This has not usually been actively urged by the new régime but has been carried out with at least the tacit consent of the officials, and the result has been to reduce the cemetery acreage from the proportions it would otherwise have reached.

In Japan, it may be observed, cremation is extensively practiced. In China the practice is followed only by Buddhists and is at present an expensive custom.

The necessity of being buried at the old home is a real one with the people of China. No matter how far afield a man may go during his lifetime, if he dies away from home his body must be brought back even though an ocean voyage is necessary. This custom coupled with that of ancestor worship furnishes an almost indissoluble tie to the particular plot of ground which has marked the abode of the family for generations, no matter how greatly its members may have increased in numbers, nor how great may have been the decrease in the fertility of the soil, nor how seriously the dependability of the crops may have been affected by the changing forces of nature through the ages. "Who will look after the graves of our ancestors?" is the question invariably asked when emigration is suggested as a source of relief.

CONSERVATISM OF THE PEOPLE

For several thousand years the life and customs of the people have been stamped in the same mold. Before the time of Confucius even, social usages and manners of life and conduct had been formed. As a matter of fact, it was Confucius' declared task to enjoin the people to follow in the footsteps of the ancients in this respect. He regarded himself not as the originator of a new social order but rather as an agent for classifying and interpreting the already existing codes laid down as the rule and guide for the conduct of future generations. Thus it is that the people of China are a backward-looking rather than a forward-looking race, and for this reason the introduction of modern ideas and practices is extremely difficult. When China achieved cultural and political solidarity her religion, social customs, and everyday manner of life were codified and became the immutable pattern for future ages. A change from former practices would indirectly imply a lack of confidence in the accepted usages laid down by those who had gone before, who are worshiped as the family divinities, and would hardly be countenanced.

It is surprising what power the simple word custom has in settling an argument. Foreigners often find it difficult to deal with servants and particularly with rickshaw men, who always demand far more than the market rate for their services. The writer has found that the simple statement "It is not my custom to give more" is the most effective method of dealing with such a situation: in almost all cases it closes the discussion.

Conservatism Delays Industrial Development

It is only since the development of machinery in the West that China has been passed in the march of material progress and fallen into the category of a backward country. Considering the splendid start which China had on the rest of the world, it is, at first glance, surprising that she did not herself learn to harness steam and electricity for the good of mankind. Why with the mental equipment possessed by the educated Chinese did they not develop a John Watt or a Thomas Edison? Those who have given the matter study are forced to conclude that it is because the value of

FIG. 59

FIG. 60

FIG. 59--Primitive power in China.   A Chinese pumping plant.
FIG. 60—The native method of lifting water for irrigation.

FIG. 61

FIG. 62

FIG. 61—In northern China donkeys carry much of the freight.
FIG. 62—In western China most of the travel is by chair.

change and progress has not been recognized, that there is no urge to experiment; the desire to do things in a more expeditious or more efficient way has not, in this most conservative country of the conservative East, been present until recently. This is quite understandable when one bears in mind the pervading quietist philosophy, the domination of established social customs and practices, and the restriction of outlook under the terrible stress of supporting life.

Education until twenty years ago followed a strict and age-worn standard, and the only path to intellectual honors was through an intimate knowledge of the classics dating back at least two millennia. Applied science was not included in the curriculum, and all the emphasis was placed on the philosophical side of learning. As some one has aptly said, "China enjoys an aristocracy of civilization." The democratization of civilization there must await the improvement of the condition of the vast peasant population.

Noncoöperation of the Chinese

The family system has greatly hindered coöperation among the people. Individualism, or rather clannishness, is probably another factor. Clan selfishness has become a national trait through the fierce struggle for existence. A limited conception of the power of united effort in these days of huge combinations of capital, and of organized endeavor in business and in politics is one of the chief things that prevents China from successfully adopting Western institutions. A number of experiments have been made, but only a few have had any measure of success. The great difficulty has been with the management of the undertaking, and most of the failures have been due to lack of what in the West would be called integrity. The managing director does not always abscond with the funds of the concern, although this sometimes happens. More usually he gets the affairs of the company entangled with his private interests. His family, as soon as his appointment is announced, saddles him with its unemployed members, and he reorganizes the business to give place on the staff for his relatives. Incidentally, greater efficiency is probably possible under this plan, for individuals do not work well together unless there are family ties. The great danger is that the director will load up the business with a much larger staff than is necessary or supportable. Probably the universal custom of peculation, recognized under the old patriarchal government and still practiced, also does much to weaken the sense of public obligation.

Noncoöperation Retards Famine Prevention

Not only does this noncoöperative spirit retard progress in the country, through preventing more rapid industrial development and exploitation of China's natural wealth, but it makes itself felt in other affairs of life, which perhaps even more intimately touch the subject of famine. Take, for instance, the development of irrigation, the building and maintenance of dikes, and the construction and repair of highways. These are all projects which would assist in preventing famines. They are, likewise, projects which can be developed by community enterprise. But they are seldom undertaken except under official auspices.

The writer has been over many stretches of almost impassable road which could easily be repaired in a few days of the leisure time of the near-by residents. But nothing is done; the villagers sit idly at home unless, perchance, they themselves are forced to drive an unwilling mule and overloaded cart over the stretch of bad road. An inquiry as to why the road was not mended would elicit the reply from the villagers that it was not their business to do it. It probably is the duty of the local official. But were pressure brought to bear on this functionary to make the necessary repairs (for instance, to smooth the way for a visit of a higher official) he would no doubt make them by impressing the very villagers who declared that it was not their duty to do the work.

It would seem to the casual foreign observer that in China nobody offers help to anybody else unless he is under some particular obligation. If a fruit peddler falls down in the street and spills his load nobody helps him to pick up his scattered goods, although probably many will stop to witness his misfortune and to watch his efforts. If a horse falls on a slippery hill, it is the duty of the driver alone to get him up. Even if a man falls and injures himself so severely that he is unable to proceed on his way, no stranger steps forward to lend him a helping hand. If there is a policeman near by it is his duty of course to assist. Under the old Chinese system any person who involves himself in another's misfortune, may be held responsible for it and be arrested by the police when they arrive on the scene. Such a prospect, it must be acknowledged, is enough to discourage the most ardent Good Samaritan.

This does not mean that the Chinese are not a charitable people. The passer-by, indifferently watching the frantic efforts of the fruit seller to gather up his wares, would probably at once respond to the appeal of a beggar. But this is the recognized thing to do; the other is not. The noncoöperative instinct is evidence of the extremely keen struggle for existence, and it is one of the reasons for China's present condition.

It should not be assumed that the Chinese are incapable of coöperating. The solidarity of the family would at once dispel any doubt on this score. Then again, the famous guilds of China, which probably had their beginning in the Chou Dynasty before the Christian era, evidence a capacity for organization that is truly superior. The Chinese have, however, given their whole allegiance to their family, their clan, or in some instances to their guild without considering that they have any obligation to community or country. Indeed, the affairs of the community or the state are not regarded as the business of the individual but only of the government or the agents of the government.

F<small>IG</small>. 63—In Szechwan.   Rice is the staple food of central and south China.

CHAPTER V

ECONOMIC CURES FOR FAMINE

In approaching a consideration of the cures for China's famines it should be borne in mind that it is only the chronic condition that can be controlled.   No one who has studied the situation in China today believes that the problem of the occasional severe food shortage resulting from some unusual catastrophe can be solved for many years to come, assuming that the population remains as large as it is at present and that new and yet undiscovered means of production are not brought to light and utilized.   But for the local disasters that occur with ever-increasing frequency there is most decidedly a cure.   Stated in its briefest form, one of the most important elements of this cure is a general improvement in the people's standard of living and the creation of an economic reserve upon which they may draw in time of need.

China has not always been as poor as she is today.   In fact, the writer is of the opinion that the living conditions of the common people have seldom if ever been as hard as now.   A prolonged series of crop failures would find the country both economically and politically less prepared to meet the resulting famine than at almost any previous time; and the records tell us that prolonged droughts, which work the greatest havoc, recur with disheartening regularity.

In almost every dynasty there has been a period of comparative prosperity when the people have had enough to eat and have enjoyed freedom from famine, except after particularly disastrous natural calamities.   It is interesting to note, however, the great difference between the population of the prosperous periods in the last two dynasties and the population today. The golden age of the Mings was just after the middle of the sixteenth century, and, according to the estimate of the China Year Book, the population at that time was only about sixty millions. During the last dynasty the most prosperous conditions were enjoyed while Ch'ien Lung occupied the throne shortly after the middle of the eighteenth century. In this interval of two hundred years the population, according to the same authority, had increased to approximately one hundred and fifty millions. Now, it is believed, there are more than four hundred million people to be supported, and the total area of the country is less than during either of the periods mentioned above, for Korea, Cochin China, Formosa, and other large land divisions have been lost to China. This increase in the number of mouths to be fed may explain why the period between disasters is becoming shorter and shorter. In Shensi province the historical records report famine conditions on the average once every twenty years before the beginning of the Ming Dynasty in 1368 A. D. and once every ten years since that time. During these five and a half centuries the population of China has multiplied seven-fold. Japan, China's nearest great neighbor, has reached the point where she has not sufficient home-grown products to feed her people; and it is the writer's opinion that the legitimate food requirements of the Chinese are not now being met in spite of the fact that the value of her food imports is, on the average, nearly 20 per cent higher than that of her exports.

The following figures on the import and export of foodstuffs have been deduced from the Maritime Customs Trade Statistics and include the last three years for which data are available:

Year	Exports	Imports
1921	$164,000,000	$167,000,000
1922	176,000,000	213,000,000
1923	212,000,000	248,000,000

These totals include living animals and food of all kinds as well as beverages. Allowing for the grain smuggled out of the country it would still seem probable that imports would be greater than exports. And thus, since a large part of the people are undernourished, it appears that China as well as Japan is not now self-supporting. This does not, of course, mean that she could not support herself if her resources were properly developed.

Scientific Agriculture

Even without enlarging the area of cultivated land, the production of foodstuffs could undoubtedly be increased by adoption of modern methods where they are shown to produce better results than the old practices as, for instance, in a more scientific rotation of crops or the utilization of more efficient plows and cultivating machinery. The schools of the country are not unmindful of these advantages, and many of them are laying greater emphasis on scientific agriculture. The greatest difficulty experienced has been in getting graduates to use their knowledge in a practical rather than a theoretical way. In China it is not customary for an educated man to engage in manual work of any sort. Farmers' sons who have had the advantage of going away to school do not return to the farm after finishing their agricultural course but seek an opportunity to teach; and many of them who fail in finding such employment drift into other lines of work where their special training is lost but where their dignity as men of education is preserved. In the current language, they have developed into "silk gown" men.

The teaching of modern agriculture is at present confined for the most part to institutions of higher learning, a plan that further encourages this divorcement from the land. In the case of missionary schools where a foreign language is taught, a large proportion of graduates, even those who have had the advantage of specialization, accept positions with foreign institutions or business firms. If modern methods are to be widely introduced, up-to-date agriculture must be taught in the lower schools, and students who have had the advantage of such training must return to the farm where they can make use of their knowledge and spread it in their community. The Chinese farmer is not impressed with theories nor willing to try new ideas unless they have been demonstrated to his satisfaction to be effective. One can thoroughly sympathize with this trait when it is recalled

FIG. 64—Famine refugees. These people had no economic reserve.

that individual holdings are, for the most part, small and that the family's food supply for the year is dependent on the success of the crop. A crop failure might mean starvation, and the average man cannot afford to take chances.

While one recognizes the great achievement of the Chinese in maintaining the fertility of the soil by their methods of fertilization, it is undoubtedly true that the introduction of chemical fertilizers would improve some of the crops. This is a matter receiving the attention of agricultural schools where laboratory work is being carried out; but it will be necessary to take the message to the man on the land and to carry out a demonstration before his very eyes. Furthermore, the Chinese farmer cannot afford anything but the cheapest available fertilizer without the extension of credit. The introduction of better credit facilities would also permit the use of better farm equipment.

INTRODUCTION OF NEW FOOD CROPS

About thirty-five years ago a foreign missionary residing in China tried the experiment of introducing peanuts. It was found that they grew finely, and it was not long before a large section of Shantung province, where the soil was

FIG. 65—Cowhide rafts are used for freight to shoot the rapids on the upper Yellow River.

sandy and considered of little use, began to yield an ever increasing harvest of this crop. At present they not only form a recognized item in the diet of the Chinese, but the export of peanuts and peanut cake has grown to surprising proportions. This crop is now grown in every province, and in 1923 the value of exports alone, which is but a fraction of the total production, amounted to nearly ten million dollars, United States currency. Since peanuts grow in sandy soil, which is considered of little use, this crop represents almost a clear gain in production.

The introduction of sweet and Irish potatoes and American corn has proved of even greater importance. Potatoes have become the staple vegetables for the poorer classes in some of the northern provinces and together with corn have taken a recognized place in the diet of the people. It is thought

that these foods, comparatively new for the Chinese, were
introduced from the Philippines, where they were first raised
by the Spaniards, probably in the latter part of the seven-
teenth century, and that the increase in production made
possible by the adoption of these new crops has been a factor
in the great growth in population since that time.

THE SOY BEAN

A striking example of the introduction and utilization of
new crops may be seen in the case of the soy bean. Until
recent years, beans and bean products have not occupied
a place of importance in commerce, although they have been
used as an article of food by the Chinese for centuries past.
It is chiefly due to experiments of the Japanese that the value
of the by-products has been established. In addition to
the tremendous quantity of beans consumed locally every
year as food, the value of the exports of this product alone
totals many tens of millions of dollars annually. Modern
Manchuria may be said to have been built on the soy bean.

The principal commercial articles derived from this
commodity are bean oil and bean cake. Bean oil is used
by both the Japanese and the Chinese, in the form of sauce
and for cooking purposes, as a base for soap making, as a
lubricant, and as an ingredient of printing ink and lacquer.
Bean cake is used as a fertilizer and in some cases as food for
cattle. Bean curd is a staple article of diet in China, and
there are literally scores of other by-products of the utmost
importance to humanity. The soy bean is in fact a new
universal provider.

It is the tremendous possibilities of this product as a food
that concern us most intimately in a discussion of famine.
Nearly fifty years ago it was predicted by an Austrian
scientist that soy beans would eventually play a very important rôle in the diet of the human race; but it was not
until the Great War caused a scarcity of food that a thorough
examination of their possibilities was undertaken, chiefly
by German specialists. Ten years ago the soy bean was

proclaimed the "culture plant of the future," and great progress has been made in developing it. Dr. A. A. Horvath of the Peking Union Medical College, in a discussion of this product, has stated that it contains all the elements necessary for normal growth and that its protein appears to be quite as valuable as the casein of milk. It is the only known seed meeting these requirements.

One of the chief merits of the bean is its cheapness. The market price for an equivalent of one hundred calories of beef is thirty times as great as for one hundred calories of the beans. Soy bean flour has been prepared by the Hungarian food physiologist, Dr. L. Berczeller, who has patented the process. The nutritive value of one pound of the flour is equal to two pounds of meat plus one-quarter pound of wheat flour; but the price is only one-twelfth of the corresponding cost for meat.

The bean flour is not a substitute for wheat flour but is a natural vegetable complement which can be substituted for expensive animal foodstuffs and lower the living rates of humanity to a degree not to be successfully reached either by the use of potatoes or maize or by intensive farming. Since the Chinese are not a meat-eating people, the soy bean will not serve them as a meat substitute; but its high nutritive value and low price will make possible its substitution for a portion of the grain which is now the staple, and almost the only, variety of food.

Although soy beans are grown in various parts of China, the crop reaches its greatest commercial value in Manchuria. It is said that this region produces 70 per cent of the world's output, and vast stretches of untenanted, cultivable lands still are available there. Proper encouragement of the cultivation of the soy bean and its adoption into the diet of the Chinese masses will do much to assist in meeting the food problem of the future.

There are probably many other foreign products that would thrive in China, for almost every variety of climate is here represented—from the cold, dry region in the north to the central provinces, which have a heavy rainfall, and the almost tropical belt in the far south. Plants may be found that will grow on land now considered of little use; others may prove economically more practical than those now cultivated and will replace them; and still others may be grown as auxiliary crops during a part of the year when the land, under present conditions, may be out of use.

Plant and Animal Improvement

It would appear that the Chinese farmers have not discovered and applied those laws of heredity that make for improvement in agriculture. By careful seed selection the University of Nanking has recently doubled the yield of corn over the fields from which the original seeds were taken, and this was accomplished in four years. A variety of wheat selected from a native field has been found that is superior to eighty other Chinese and imported varieties and that gives a yield of forty bushels to the acre.

It is not only the growing of larger food crops that will assist in preventing famine, but the improvement of other products will result in greater wealth, and this wealth can in turn be exchanged abroad for food. The growing of better cotton, the production of more readily marketable silk,[27] and the better culture of tea will all have the effect of improving China's economic status. It was China that first gave silk and tea to the world; but other countries have so greatly improved these products that Chinese goods have been left behind in quality and far behind, consequently, in markets. Japan has outstripped her in the exportation of the better grade of raw silk; and China's tea trade is now but a shadow of what it was sixty to eighty years ago. India and Ceylon have had little difficulty in capturing the foreign market for the common cheaper varieties. This is due to the fact that the traditional Chinese methods of cultivation are not based on scientific knowledge.

[27] An encouraging recognition of the need for improvement may be seen in a survey of the silk industry of southern China by the Department of Sericulture of Canton Christian College (Ling Nan Agricultural College), the results of which are published as *Agricultural Bulletin No. 12*, Canton, 1925.

Insect pests and plant diseases cause famine only indirectly by decreasing the yield of foodstuffs. The preventable losses occurring under both these heads, however, are truly enormous. One example will suffice. In northern Chekiang an insect pest called Min Chung has been found to work great havoc on the rice crop. It eats its way into the stem of the rice ears, causing them to die before the kernels are fully developed. The *Chinese Economic Bulletin* in a recent issue published an estimate of the losses from this insect. In 1924 the crops in six counties, of a total area of approximately 640,000 acres, were damaged to the extent of more than $13,000,000, Chinese currency. This is about $20 an acre.[28]

ECONOMIC VALUE OF TREE PLANTING

There are literally millions of acres of worthless land where valuable forests might now be growing to provide China with timber, to relieve agriculture of the necessity of supplying fuel to the population, and to assist in improving the economic status of the people and so furnishing them with a margin to meet the periods of failing crops. That the raising of trees for their wood alone is a profitable enterprise has been proved. The writer in traveling from Tungkwan to Sian in Shensi province saw great numbers of wood lots along the valley of the Wei River. This area is composed of extremely rich agricultural land and is densely populated; but wood is so valuable that it pays to substitute cottonwood trees for other crops. Irrigation is practiced extensively in this district, and it is customary to grow cottonwoods along the sides of the irrigation canals. An extension of these practices to other provinces might well be carried out.

The raising of fruit-bearing trees would provide additional food, which could be eaten in times of crop failure and in good years could be dried or preserved against the day of want.

Because of the shade they cast and the nourishment they take from the soil, it is not likely that trees can be grown to

[28] *Chinese Econ. Monthly*, Vol. 8, No. 256, Chinese Govt. Bur. of Econ. Information. Peking.

any extent on the plains. Also the great scarcity of fuel makes the protection of the young trees a much more difficult matter on the lowlands than in the hills where the pressure of population is not so great and where there is usually some grass or underbrush which can be garnered to meet the more pressing needs of the people for fuel.

Most of the plains, particularly in northern China, are subject to inundation. When the drainage from the flooded areas is slow it ofttimes happens that winter overtakes the inhabitants before the water has left their land, and the fuel supply in the form of kaoliang stalks and roots, straw, bean and sweet potato vines, etc., is buried under a sheet of ice. Thus whole districts find themselves suddenly without fuel enough to cook their food, and then what trees there are must be sacrificed, regardless of their degree of maturity.

During the winter of 1924–1925 the writer made a trip from Paotingfu to Tientsin to inspect the region inundated by the floods of the previous summer. Almost the entire distance of about a hundred miles was made by ice boat, and the route lay over the flooded crops of the farmers. A region of several thousand square miles was covered by a sheet of ice (Fig. 53): scarcely a tree or blade of grass was visible, excepting along one of the main dikes where trees had been planted to strengthen it against erosion, and these presented a pitiful sight. The smaller trees were for the most part broken off, leaving a stump two or three feet in height. The larger ones had lost their limbs not in any regular way nor by saw or axe, but by a process of tearing; and, in a few instances, some rude implement had been used to hack at the trunks of the larger ones in a vain effort to fell them. One was reminded of the scarred and shattered remnants of the trees of the Argonne Forest in France after several years of war.

Among the hilly regions where the slopes are too steep for cultivation lie the best possibilities for forestation; but in these regions great labor is necessary, especially at the start; for the young trees must be watered for the first two or three years, and water is usually scarce and must be

Fig. 66

Fig. 67

Fig. 66—Refugees from Chihli floods of 1924 living on dikes.   (Photograph by Lawrence Impey.)

Fig. 67—In flood times many families take to boats.

carried up from the valleys. This prodigious labor probably discourages the natives, especially when the returns are delayed for a number of years, and in fact, may not accrue during a lifetime. But the solidarity of the family is such that if something in the nature of family wood lots could be established and the economic benefits of such projects demonstrated, the impetus given to tree planting would in course of time contribute much towards the relief of China's wood shortage.

COLONIZATION TO RELIEVE OVERCROWDING

If the population of China were redistributed to relieve the densely crowded provinces of their burden, a cure for chronic famine conditions could be effected by this means alone. The cure would last at least until the plains again became overpopulated, a circumstance which, if present conditions continue, would unfortunately happen again in the course of time. But the opening up of thousands of square miles of good farm lands would afford a considerable breathing space and meanwhile a change in customs might result from the introduction of industrialism or from other causes and gradually decrease the present high birth rate. It is a scientific fact that comfort and prosperity militate against human fertility quite apart from the development of a habit of voluntary control.

Although parts of China are so congested, still there remain vast stretches of sparsely settled arable land. Most of this land is in Mongolia and Manchuria, which furnish the best areas for colonization; but, even among the provinces constituting what is still commonly known as China proper, there are several that could accommodate much larger numbers. In Yunnan, Kweichow, Kansu, and Kwangsi there is ample room for a larger population. These provinces comprise nearly 28 per cent of the total area of China proper, but their population is less than 10 per cent of the total. Manchuria, with an area 24 per cent as large as China proper, has only about 5 per cent of the population. Mongolia, with

1,370,000 square miles, is nearly 90 per cent as large as the original eighteen provinces but has only one-half of 1 per cent of its population. It is only the fringe of Mongolia, however, that is habitable for man. Chinese Turkestan and Tibet are also vast areas which are more or less open to the settlement of Chinese, although climatic and other geographic considerations make a large movement of emigrants to these far-away territories difficult if not impossible. The most accessible regions next to the four provinces of China proper mentioned above are Inner Mongolia and Manchuria.

The adventurous spirit that settled the western part of North America is entirely lacking in China. Conditions may be considered in some degree analogous to those of the United States in the nineteenth century. There are fertile sparsely settled regions, but there are also hardships and dangers to be overcome if they are to be occupied. In America it was the Indians, in China it is the bandits that must be dealt with. Climatic conditions, too, are different in Mongolia and Manchuria, where the best lands are. The winters are cold and long, and agricultural methods successful on the great eastern plains will not produce the same results farther north. But the great factor against Chinese emigration is the innate conservatism of the race coupled with a lack of proper governmental encouragement and support. The well known American slogan, "Young man, go west," has no counterpart in China; in fact, the common proverbs stress rather the desirability of a quiet life at home and compare such security and serenity with the perils and discomforts to be met in traveling abroad. Not that the colonization movement is altogether lacking. For many years there has been an advance of the Chinese farmer into Manchuria and Mongolia. Mr. Dudley Buxton estimates it at an average of a mile a year for the last 50 years over a considerable front.[29] But those who go are few by the side of the millions who remain at home. Likewise the emigration movement overseas has afforded no appreciable relief to the pressure of popula-

[29] The Eastern Road, pp. 144–145.

tion. The total number of Chinese now residing abroad
has been estimated at not much over 8,000,000.[30]

It will take outside pressure to break down the conservatism of the Chinese, particularly of the Northerners,
who cling to their old homes with a tenacity born of twenty
or thirty centuries of tradition.

Migration During Famine

But there are times when such outside pressure automatically comes into play. During famine periods large
numbers of people migrate. Apparently there has never
been any attempt to direct this migration in such wise
that the people whose home ties have been severed will settle
in a region where there is a possibility of permanently better
conditions of life. It has been the custom to discourage
people from moving and to feed them at or near their homes;
and, unless a carefully prepared plan is followed and provision
made to support the wandering families in the colonization
region, this course is much the better one. As a general
rule the wanderers do not get far, and those who manage
to survive eventually find their way back to the old home.
But the relief given by the government and other agencies
might as conveniently be extended in districts that are
suitable for colonization and the wandering people led or
transported to such places. The assistance given them would
then tide them over until their first crop was harvested just
the same as if they had remained at home.

Certainly this method is not as cheap as the old practice
of distributing grain in the famine belt, nor is it nearly so
easy. But it has the unquestionable advantage of providing
effective and lasting relief for the overcrowded condition
that is at the root of the famine evil.

It is not proposed that all the families in a famine-affected
district should be moved. The idea is to ascertain, when it
becomes evident that there will be a severe famine, what
number of people should or could be moved; then, when the

[30] Ta Chen: Chinese Migrations, with Special Reference to Labor Conditions,
Bull. U. S. Bur. of Labor Statistics No. 340, Washington, *1923*.

pressure for food is severe enough so that families will consent
to migrate, to move them out.   If the movement is started
in time, it will relieve the congestion in the affected districts,
and what food is available will go further toward meeting
needs.   The railways which bring in loaded cars of grain will
not take them back as empties, but filled with the emigrants
and their belongings.

The most needy families—those which have no land or
at least very small holdings—will be the first to emigrate,
and the community will be relieved of the necessity of supporting them in future emergencies.   The land of those who
move out can be held until the famine is over and conditions
have become normal and then sold to others in the district
and the proceeds credited to the former owner, who in the
meantime can be given a potentially more valuable holding
in the new district.

Such a method of relief requires good organization, assistance from or close coöperation with government officials,
and honest administration.   One is constrained to wonder
what changes in the conditions of the districts most severely
affected by the 1920–1921 famine would have resulted from
the use in such a way of the $37,000,000 expended in relief.
It will be recalled that most of this sum was distributed for
free relief.   The utilization of famine relief funds for colonization purposes in times of distress is, however, to be regarded
only an adjunct of a permanent government colonization
scheme.

THE "FRONTIER MOVEMENT"

With the so-called awakening of China and the knowledge
of what has been accomplished in other countries, there is
a growing tendency for the people themselves to attack some
of these huge economic problems along modern lines.   The
"frontier movement," sponsored by Dr. Yu Tinn Hugh,
is probably one of the best-known projects dealing with this
question of the movement of population from overcrowded
to sparsely settled regions.   It is primarily an educational
scheme, designed especially to spread a knowledge of the

benefits that colonization will bring to the individual and the country. But to be effective it must be coördinated with some definite organization having a plan and ample funds to provide the necessary capital for the colonizers to start them in their new homes. In the North and Northwest

FIG. 68—A settler's temporary quarters on Feng Yu-hsiang's colonization scheme in the Northwest.

there is but one crop a year; and, if the people are moved during the winter, they must be supported until the following fall and in addition have enough capital to buy seed and a few simple farm implements and perhaps live stock.

COLONIZATION COMPANIES

Another innovation which has possibilities is the organization of colonization companies. These are formed primarily as money-making ventures. One or more capitalists will secure a large tract of land in virgin fields and offer certain inducements to settlers. This generally includes sufficient capital to carry them until the first crop is harvested. Thereafter, a certain proportion of each crop is turned over to the colonization company. For the most part, these schemes have not proved successful, for the company's purpose is to make money, and in the beginning the returns are slow. It is difficult to make the colonists stay. After all the land is not their own, the winters are long and hard, they are far from what they regard as home, and in a strange environment. It needs the assurance of unusual returns to hold men under such circumstances. Furthermore, as the

Fig. 69—The motor road between Kalgan and Kansu built by General Feng Yu-hsiang was kept clear of bandits by his troops.

colonization companies are simply concerned with labor, they only take families because they believe that such a course will result in a larger degree of contentment on the part of the men and consequently in a smaller labor turnover.

Both colonization companies and the "frontier movement" are beneficial, however, even though they do not make sufficiently radical changes to bring effective relief for overcrowding. They encourage a tendency toward change, they assist in spreading the knowledge that there are places where conditions of life are less severe, and they prepare the way for a greater and more comprehensive movement of population which may eventually bring the desired and much-needed relief for China's overcrowding.

One of the discouraging features of the present colonization tendencies is the lack of security in the bandit-infested regions of Manchuria and Mongolia. When any community has had a good crop or has succeeded in amassing any quantity of worldly goods, these bands of outlaws swoop down upon it, carry off everything of value that is movable, and perhaps even hold a few of the leading citizens for ransom. An American colonization company in Manchuria, which after several years' operation was just beginning to prove successful, was recently raided and the American manager lost his life. It is this reason which makes necessary the effective coöperation of the officials.

The Experiments of General Feng Yu-hsiang

An official colonization project of recent years is that undertaken by Marshal Feng Yu-hsiang, commonly called the Christian General. Marshal Feng is one of China's conspicuous military leaders, having figured prominently in nearly all the civil wars since 1922. After serving as Governor of Shensi and Honan, he moved his troops in 1923 to Peking, where they have been in virtual control ever since. After the war of 1924 he established himself in Kalgan and was officially recognized as the Governor General of the Northwest. This territory includes Inner Mongolia and provides one of the best areas for settlement. The Peking-Suiyuan Railway makes these districts readily accessible, and General Feng early saw the benefits possible from bringing into the area new settlers from the crowded provinces of Shantung and Chihli.

His first step was to move about a thousand heads of families from Shantung to the new country in order that they might see for themselves what conditions were like before bringing their entire households. Although no official reports have been made on the subject, it is believed that only a small portion of this number remained during the first winter, the others getting disheartened and returning to their old homes. This was a sufficiently discouraging start, but a much more serious setback occurred to the scheme when, after his successful campaign against Tientsin, Feng suddenly resigned all his offices and went into retirement, turning over his duties to his subordinates. Undoubtedly this will break the continuity of the colonization plan, for if the Christian General's military organization falls to pieces other officials with different ideas will take over the control of the Northwest and the scheme of colonization may be given up entirely.

This instance shows in a striking way the necessity for the control of such projects by an effective central Government, where plans which have been carefully prepared may have a chance of being followed through year after year regardless of any changes in local officials.

INDUSTRIAL DEVELOPMENT

The industrial development of China will do much to take care of the excess labor that is at present such a burden to the land. The opening of factories in the principal ports has already had a noticeable effect in neighboring districts, and an appreciable improvement in living standards has followed. The opening of mines, the construction of railroads, and other developments making available to China and the world the latent wealth of this great country will provide employment for increasing numbers, and the results of their toil will be to afford the masses greater conveniences and more of the comforts of life. Incidentally, the exportation of the products of China's mineral resources, either in the raw state or as manufactured articles, will provide credits abroad for the importation of foodstuffs. In the writer's opinion, however, it will not be necessary to import food unless the population increases considerably. China's undernourishment is due, as has been pointed out before, in part to the poor distribution of crops which better transportation would rectify. The betterment of economic conditions would provide capital for improving agriculture.

The establishment of an export trade in manufactured articles will be a difficult matter for years to come, for, with Japan as a neighbor, the capture of foreign markets will not be easy. Eventually, however, with China's superior natural resources, the time may come when she will find it possible to meet the Western powers and Japan on their own ground. Meanwhile, raw materials may be sold abroad in ever-increasing quantities, and there is sufficient home market to take the output of as many factories as the limited capital of the country permits. This latter aspect of the matter, the supply of the home market, does not seem yet to have dawned on those publicists who fear China's competition in the race for markets. Industrialization will march hand in hand with increased purchasing power, whose possibilities, as Sir Edwin Stockton, a leading British business man, has pointed out, are magical.[31]

FIG. 70—Irrigation from a stream in northern China. (Photograph by Hartung.)

A comparison of the enumerated articles listed by the Maritime Customs a decade ago with those of the current year shows that the Chinese are demanding from foreign markets more and more commodities that were formerly foreign to their taste and that have gradually become necessities. This demand is due partly to the economic improvement of the people and partly to the keen desire of the present-day Chinese to share in the cosmopolitan fruits of modern invention and industry.

The late Wu Ting-fang once said, and Lord Riddell has recently made a similar comment, that if one could succeed in adding an inch to the shirt tail of every Chinese, the cotton mills of the world would be kept busy for years in supplying the increased demand. This is a facetious comment on the

[31] *Financial News*, January 14, 1926, London.

apparent inexhaustibility of the Chinese market, once purchasing power approximates that in Western countries.
There are still millions of Chinese who are not provided with
the ordinary requirements of life and whose shirts are merely
patches of cloth disguised as garments. It is not to be pre-
sumed, therefore, that a home industry, no matter how intense its development, will be
able to cope unaided with
home demands. Rather, with
the betterment in the economic position of the Chinese
as a result of the industrialization of the country, the demand on foreign markets will
pursue its present upward
trend until China becomes in
fact a 400-million-purchasing-
power country, whose requirements the mills of the whole
world will be competing to
supply.

And in addition to the advantage derived from China's
expanded buying power, the
industrial countries of the
West are reaping benefits in
the disposal of machinery
and equipment to her infant
industries.

FIG. 71—A native pile driver.

HOME AND VILLAGE INDUSTRY

Probably as great benefits to the individual during the
next few years can be secured through the development of
home and village industries as will accrue from the few larger
projects that may be initiated. There are several reasons
why the utilization of the idle time of the rural population
at their homes would be preferable to the removal of these

people to the cities. These reasons are for the most part of a social nature, the usual problems that attend the massing of large numbers in an industrial center.

No country can compete with China in turning out products where the principal cost of production is for direct labor. In the interior able-bodied men will work a twelve-hour day for but the equivalent of fifteen or twenty cents, American money. Even first-class artisans get very little more, and women are not able to earn even this much in most cases. Thus it is that lace making has progressed by leaps and bounds of late years, as has also the exportation of hand-embroidered silks and linens and objects of art. Most of these products are suited to village manufacture. They are not too bulky for easy distribution, and they can be made on a piece-work basis, thus utilizing the spare time of the people. The extension of this form of village industry is almost limitless in its possibilities and is much to be desired. Although some capital would be necessary, the sum would be much smaller than that required for mass production by machine methods.

There are also some enterprises suitable for country districts where machines of a simple nature may be employed. The introduction of hand looms, for instance, has furnished a new source of income to rural communities in Chihli province, which has been of inestimable benefit to the people. These looms are simple in construction and cheap. The yarn is furnished by the large dealers, who in turn take the finished product at specified prices. The cloth that is made has a ready market, for it is designed for local consumption.

A concrete example of the growth of an enterprise of this sort is the knitting of hosiery introduced into Chekiang about ten years ago. Where at first a few machines were rented out to the villagers, there are now almost 10,000 owned by many companies. It is estimated that the machines are 80 per cent efficient, and each machine operated by a housewife in her spare time will produce a dozen pairs of stockings daily.

Better Credit Facilities

One of the greatest needs of rural China is a provision of credit at rates of interest that will make borrowing beneficial. The territory comprising the twenty-two provinces is so large and has such a range of climate that it is practically impossible for the crops to fail over the whole country. The problem that presents itself is to find a means of providing the credit that would make possible the purchase of the excess of the yield in the fortunate districts by the afflicted people in the famine belt.

It has already been explained that the banks, which are of necessity located in the cities, are not easily able to make loans to individuals in the villages. Obviously any credit arrangement must have as one of its principal features the careful oversight of each loan, and this means that some purely local agency must be in a position to know intimately the character and condition of the prospective borrowers. This is particularly necessary when the loan is desired for some constructive enterprise, the repayment to be made from the expected profits. And it is, of course, a prime requisite when no security beyond the integrity of the individual borrower is offered. The maintenance of such an agency by the banks would more than eat up the profits from transactions undertaken.

Coöperative Credit Societies

The Famine Commission, which early saw the great need for rural credits and carried out a thorough study of the subject, has found a solution in the experience of Western countries—a solution which, in the writer's opinion, will in a few years revolutionize the present credit practices of China. This idea was none other than the rural coöperative credit scheme devised by Raiffeisen in Germany in 1848, which it is interesting to note arose out of the serious famine conditions of that time. Briefly, this plan provides for the banding together of individuals in rural communities for the purpose of obtaining loans from outside sources on the

joint security of the members, each of which accepts unlimited liability for the actions of all the rest. The funds
so received are reloaned to the members at a slightly higher
rate, the difference serving to build up a reserve fund.

This is a singularly simple device, but it meets almost
ideally the needs of rural China. The men who join such a
society are all known to one another, and, since each must
agree to assume any undischarged obligations of any of the
other members, the unreliable or otherwise undesirable
elements in the community are automatically eliminated.
The intimate knowledge possessed by the members about
the affairs of all the others provides personal security only
as the basis of loans. This intimate knowledge also makes
possible the unlimited liability which is the greatest factor
in convincing the lending bank of the integrity of the society.
The localization of the group and their mutual knowledge
insure a careful inspection of the uses to which the individual
loans are put.

While the banks are unable to do business with the individual farmer on a profitable basis for either party, the combined business of a group of perhaps forty or fifty is worth
their while. The joint security of the members of the credit
society obviates the necessity of investigation, and the rate
of interest need not, therefore, be higher than for ordinary
business transactions in the cities.

The organization of the societies provides an executive
committee elected by and from its membership, each member
having one vote. This committee has the power of making
loans to the individual members from the society's funds.
Since loans can be contracted only for specific purposes,
there is elected, also, a council of inspection, whose duty
it is to see that funds advanced are devoted exclusively to
the purpose named. All the officers and committees serve
without remuneration. Thus the societies are run at practically no cost. Money is borrowed from outside and reloaned to members, inspection is made, books and records
are kept, and all the operations of the society are carried
out by the members themselves.

A new credit idea, even one which has proved successful in other countries, must be demonstrated to be thoroughly effective before it is taken up by so conservative a group as bankers. This is particularly so in China. The Famine Commission soon realized that a demonstration would have to be made altruistically. After a detailed study of the methods employed in other countries, a model plan of organization adapted to Chinese requirements was drawn up and sufficient funds were allocated for the experiment. At first the progress was designedly slow; after more than three years' operation, there are less than a hundred recognized societies to which a total of approximately $50,000 has been loaned, the Famine Commission acting as the central bank. The project is still considered to be in the experimental stage, but its success can be foreseen. Not a society has defaulted in making repayment. The societies contain many hundred members, most of whom have received advances, and no member had defaulted up to the time of writing. The banks are already beginning to be impressed with the stability of the societies.

Coöperative societies will eventually be organized in all the provinces, and, when they are linked together by a central bank, one of the greatest famine-prevention agencies will have been formed. Ultimate success does not necessarily depend upon government assistance, although this would greatly stimulate the movement, as it has done in India; but at least, the movement will need to be free from government interference in the form of heavy taxation or the commandeering of the resources of the bank or the societies by officials.

Given a stable government, foreign capital might be made available to augment the surplus wealth of the towns, and this would find its way into food production.

NEED OF UNIFORM COINAGE

One of the necessary aids to the free circulation of goods is a uniform coinage for the whole country. At the present time every province and even many a city in the same province has its own currency.   Nominally, each one accepts the government standard adopted in 1910, but even the silver dollar (China has a silver standard) has a different value in different parts of the country.   Following the custom of thousands of years, most of the retail business in the interior is still carried on by the use of strings of copper cash or of copper coins, each the equivalent of ten or twenty cash. The rate between coppers and silver varies from day to day. In Peking a silver dollar will now buy more than three hundred coppers.   Five years ago it bought less than half this number.

At the present time there are mints in nearly all the provinces, which are equipped to turn out silver dollars. However, they mint silver only when a profit can be realized; when no profit can be made many of them turn to copper coins or suspend operations altogether.   The government currency bureau at Peking, supposed to control all the mints, has failed to do so, and the provincial authorities have come to regard minting as a source of revenue rather than a public service.   Hence the coins that are turned out are not uniform in weight, fineness, or appearance; and many of them are good only in the province where they are made, being accepted in other provinces at a discount.

The deplorable condition of the country's currency is widely recognized.   Mr. Rodney Gilbert, writing in the *North China Herald*, August 19, 1916, puts it this way:

> If a man comes into a shop one day when 93 cash constitute a hundred, of these 93 cash 70 per cent should consist of large cash and 30 per cent small cash, and he makes a 29 cash purchase, he will readily spend an hour or so arguing with the shopkeeper as to what 70 per cent of 93 per cent of 29 is; and since the Chinese have no actual system of reckoning on paper, it must all be calculated with the ubiquitous swan pan, or "abacus."

Is it any wonder, then, seeing that a hundred cash are not a hundred cash and a thousand cash not a thousand, that the Chinese say that if you take any given sum on the street and convert it ten times, "you will have nothing left, even if you start with a million."

Numerous attempts have been made in recent years to correct this condition but without success.   A reform of the

FIG. 72

FIG. 73

FIG. 72—Native junks are becoming scarce on the Upper Yangtze.

FIG. 73—Steamers like this of the Standard Oil Company are replacing the junks on the Upper Yangtze.

currency would bring great benefits, and indirectly would affect even the famine question by stimulating trade and making the circulation of products easier.

THE MARITIME CUSTOMS

There is much talk of the desirability of increasing the tariff rates of the Maritime Customs in order to provide

Fig. 74—The extension of the Lung Hai Railroad through the loess country in western Honan.

"needed revenue for the administrative expenses of the Government," and there is at the time of writing a tariff conference in the Capital, at which China and the foreign powers are endeavoring to reach an agreement whereby China can obtain additional revenue without adversely affecting the trade of the individual nations.

Even assuming that the revenue derived from increased duties were devoted to constructive projects—a supposition open to considerable question—the wholesale increase of custom duties would work great harm. The importation of machinery, lumber, railway equipment, and all the other products on which industrial expansion depends should be encouraged rather than hampered. China is rich in raw materials, but she will not be able to use them for her own benefit or that of mankind without modern machinery.

Abolition of Interior Customs Stations

Increase in custom duties is supposed to depend on the abolition of likin, or transit taxes, in the interior. China is dotted with these barriers, all of which take their toll

Fig. 75—The native cart tracks are flooded in wet weather.

of dues on all domestic goods in transit. In 1921 the number of recognized tax barriers totaled 735, and each of these had a number of substations.[32] Foreign goods are protected by treaty from these impositions, having merely a transit tax at one point instead of many transit taxes at many points. Such, at any rate, is the theory, but in recent years the Chinese have shown a disregard for treaties with the result that foreign imported goods are handled in the same uncertain way as domestic. No one seriously believes that abolition of these obnoxious dues is possible for many years, for it would mean the voluntary relinquishment of revenue on the part of various provincial military leaders and a conse-

[32] C. K. Moser: Likin—China's Inland Trade Tax, *Commerce Repts.*, No. 23, 1926, pp. 592–595.

quent increase in the resources of the militarist who happens to control Peking and the so-called central government.

But the abolition of likin on domestic goods is more important than on imports, for the volume is much greater; and the imposts on the movement of foodstuffs from province to province is one of the direct causes of famine distress. The complete annulment of this practice is needed, not only for foreign-made articles but for all classes of goods. Such action would have a salutary effect in improving conditions. As Adam Smith wrote a hundred and fifty years ago:

> Were all nations to follow the liberal system of free exportation and free importation, the different States into which a great continent was divided would so far resemble the different provinces of a great Empire. As among the different provinces of a great Empire, the freedom of the inland trade appears, both from reason and experience, not only the best palliative of a dearth, but the most effectual preventative of a famine, so would the freedom of the exportation and importation trade be among the different States into which a great continent was divided.

BETTER TRANSPORTATION FACILITIES

The immense importance of improved communications in famine relief has been most effectually demonstrated in India. "The greatest administrative achievement of the last twenty years has been the extension of communications. Railways have revolutionized relief. The final horror of famine, an absolute dearth of food, is now unknown."[33] China's need is too evident to require more than a mere recital of the fact. Of the eighteen provinces of China proper there are still five that are entirely without railroads, and several of the provinces have but a few miles of line. In addition to this, the vast territory of Tibet and Turkestan is entirely cut off from rail communication with China proper: the existing lines originate at the eastern seaboard and extend less than five hundred miles inland from the coast. The richest and most populous province, Szechwan, is without a mile of railway, most of the trade being borne by the

[33] The Imperial Gazetteer of India: The Indian Empire, Vol. 3, Economic, new edit., Oxford, 1907, p. 482.

Fig. 76

Fig. 77

Fig. 78

Fig. 76—The Famine Commission has built more roads in China than any other single agency.

Fig. 77—Famine Commission roads are built for proper drainage.

Fig. 78—A Famine Commission motor road in Shensi with native cart road at the side.

Yangtze River, whose dangerous rapids make steam navigation difficult.

The rivers of China are for the most part unsuited for steam navigation because of their unstable channels; but many of them are navigable at certain seasons of the year, and the introduction of modern steam vessels is possible to a certain extent. The old hand-propelled junks are still carrying the bulk of China's freight, but for the transportation of food in times of emergency this method is too slow unless the stricken area lies downstream from the regions where a surplus is available. In the northern provinces the period of greatest distress is in the low-water season when many of the streams are dry, and this is particularly so when the famine is due to drought.

As a preventive of famines the first requisite is the construction of additional railways, especially trunk lines to link up the rich grain-producing provinces with the northern area where crop failures are most likely to occur. At the same time the building of roads would make the movement of supplies to and from the railheads cheaper and more expeditious. Improvement of waterways and introduction of power-driven craft where possible would complete the modernization of China's transportation system.

Good Roads Movement in China

The Famine Commission, by utilizing the able-bodied members of famine-stricken families, has built more roads in China than any other single agency. Such an impetus has been given to the road movement that a Good Roads Association has already been formed by the Chinese. In the course of the Famine Commission's labors all types of highways have been tried, and experience has confirmed the opinion of its engineers that for China's present needs the dirt road is the best—a conclusion similar to that found by the good roads movement in the Argentine. This type of road is not only cheaper than macadam but is more easily maintained. After the rainy season it is always necessary to make repairs, but with a dirt road this is a comparatively simple matter; and if in the dry season the surface is occasionally sprinkled and rolled the highway will be suitable even for motor traffic. In order to maintain it at all, however, it will be necessary to exclude the native narrow-tired carts, ideally constructed to make ruts. An effort is being made to introduce carts with wide tires which will carry a heavier load without impairing the condition of the highway; but until this can be accomplished it is probably a better policy to reserve the center part of the road for motor traffic and to build on each side and at a lower level a section for the native carts. Experience shows that an ordinary dirt road in northern China can be maintained at an annual cost of not more than fifty dollars, United States currency, a mile.

Food Conservation

The fierce struggle for existence in China has naturally led to a conservation of food. In fact, the principle has been so firmly established by the practice of generation after generation that it has become ingrained in the social customs of the people, their philosophy, and even their religion. Mention has already been made of the now abandoned government granaries, which retained the surplus of good years until they were needed in years of want; but the most important conservation practices are to be found in the social customs of the people. To waste food is a sin. There is a proverb which states that those who do not waste rice will always have rice to eat.

Meat, poultry, and fish are conserved in salt or in bean oil; vegetables and eggs are also preserved by immersing them in brine. These are, of course, household customs; and thus far very little has been done toward the keeping of food in large quantities against the day of need, excepting the old granary system mentioned in a preceding chapter. Great good can be achieved by the adoption of scientific principles of storage on a larger scale, especially for saving grain. Refrigeration for meat and fish has not yet been developed to any extent though there are one or two plants in the treaty ports. Fish forms a principal article of diet in some districts of China, and the conservation of this product by refrigeration is greatly needed.

Last year there was a large crop of potatoes in Suiyuan in Inner Mongolia. They were a drug on the local market, and a hundred pounds could be bought for about ten cents, American money. Yet at Peking, only three hundred miles away, the price was many times as great although there is a railway between the two points. This condition, due in the main to civil war, often occurs with other vegetables, and the suggestion has been made that dehydration would be a great aid to the conservation of the surplus in such instances. There are probably great possibilities in this idea, although it has not even been tried as yet in China. Dehydration greatly decreases the weight and bulk of the product; and, when one considers the difficulties of transport in China, it will be seen that such a proposal has more than one argument to recommend it.

In spite of the general thriftiness and frugality of the people there is one food that is regularly and universally wasted in China, namely fruit. Fruit does not form as important an item in the diet in China as it does in the West, probably because of the difficulty of transporting a bulky and perishable product. Better marketing facilities will help the situation, but the practice of drying the surplus or preserving it for future use will do most to conserve this item of the food supply of the country.

FIG. 79—Deforestation through centuries has resulted in scarcity of wood.

CHAPTER VI

NATURAL CURES FOR FAMINE

One is prone to believe that natural calamities are not preventable. But it is surprising how many disasters could either be averted altogether, or their dire effects mitigated, if treated scientifically and in time. It is, of course, impossible to foresee the occurrence of earthquakes, typhoons, and tidal waves in time to take preventive measures to save property or to do anything to make them happen less frequently. In fact, there is very little which can be done to lessen the severity of the consequences of such visitations of nature's wrath to the unfortunate people who are caught by them. But, fortunately, famines of a widespread nature are almost never due to natural phenomena of this category.

CURES FOR DROUGHT FAMINES: TREE PLANTING ON A LARGE SCALE

It has been said that whereas the calamitous results from too much or too concentrated rainfall can in most cases be avoided, man is not able by any means so far devised to induce rain by his own effort. There are those who believe that forests, if sufficiently wide in extent, will ensure ample and regular rainfall. But scientists are not agreed on this point. Without wishing in any way to disparage the beneficial effects which the forestation of China's barren hills would have on the country, the writer is constrained to disagree with the theory that simply by planting trees in sufficient numbers periods of drought would be prevented. Even supposing that such a course should have the desired effect, under present conditions in China it would be well-nigh impossible to carry it out.

The drought area in northern China is, for the most part, a great plain almost every foot of which is under cultivation. The only land not utilized for growing crops is that occupied by villages and grave mounds. If we must have a forest cover to "attract" rain over this vast territory, eight hundred miles long and three or four hundred miles wide, where are we going to plant the trees? Certainly no one would advocate taking good grain land out of cultivation for such a purpose. As to the mountain regions west of the plain, they present perhaps even more difficulty. The hills are so barren that no moisture is retained for any length of time. It is therefore necessary to water the young trees planted there at least twice a year for several years until they get a start. Foresters tell us that each watering requires ten gallons of water. This is the normal load for a man carrying the water up the steep slopes from the valleys below. The amount of human labor that would be required to plant enough trees to have any appreciable effect on the rainfall is beyond computation. It may be that a careful study would result in the discovery of some sort of shrub that would grow without being watered and would form sufficient cover in course of time to retain the necessary moisture to make possible the growing of trees. Only by some such device can the hills and mountains of China be wooded. But even assuming there were extensive forests in the hill country to the westward, there is no proof that a regular and ample rainfall would be secured for the plains where the moisture is needed.

We must accept the conclusion that droughts are certain to recur at intervals (assuming that no radical climatic changes introduce new factors in the situation) and must lay plans to cope with them rather than waste our efforts in a vain endeavor to change the processes of nature.

IRRIGATION OF THE CHENGTU PLAIN

The Chinese people in historic times recognized the value of irrigation, as is attested by ancient remains. One of the

Fig. 80

Fig. 81

Fig. 80—Trees in northern China proper are found only in and around the towns and villages.

Fig. 81—Tree planting in Shensi province. The young trees must be watered until they get a good start.

oldest major projects and practically the only one maintained through the centuries at maximum efficiency is the scheme that provides water to the Chengtu plain in Szechwan province. The enterprise, which dates back to the fourth century before Christ, is recognized as a great engineering feat, and Western experts have marveled that it could have been carried out in days when the science of engineering was practically unknown; they even say that there is much to learn today from a careful study of this project.

Chinese history tells us that the Chengtu plain, which comprises an area 3500 square miles in extent, was originally a barren waste unfit for human habitation because of its aridity. The provision of water has converted the region into a land of plenty supporting in prosperity a population estimated at 6,000,000. It is referred to as "the Garden of Western China" and produces a rice crop which never fails.[34]

Briefly the scheme consists in the distribution of the rushing waters of the Min River over the whole plain. This is effected through a diversion of the stream, at the point where it emerges from the hills, into a network of canals. The work took many years to execute and has been improved and extended at various times since its inception. It is necessary every year to clean the silt from the canals, and in order to dry the channels a dam is constructed in the late winter and removed in the spring. Many dams or weirs are constructed along the main watercourses, and Persian wheels are used to lift the water from the canals onto the fields.

OTHER OLD IRRIGATION PROJECTS

The old Chinese irrigation schemes of any size are usually situated along streams where they emerge from the hills, the lack of efficient pumping machinery making it necessary to put the water on the land by gravity alone. The construction of dams for storage against the dry season and for raising the water level so that a large area could be covered, was a difficult matter for the ancients. This was usually

[34] *Chinese Econ. Monthly*, Vol. 2, No. 7, Chinese Govt. Bur. of Econ. Information. Peking.

accomplished by carrying the intake for the canal far up into the hills and leading the water in a channel along the course of the river but with a lower gradient so that it came out high up on the plain.

A good example of an ancient native scheme is to be found on the Wei-pei plain of Shensi province. There are five rivers crossing this plain, and three of them have been used for irrigation. The oldest works were constructed toward the end of the Chou Dynasty, more than two thousand years ago. According to history, this and the Chengtu scheme were the first large projects carried out in China. Water was taken from the King River which is at the northwestern corner of the plain and led in a main canal along the foothills in an easterly direction. Lateral canals at frequent intervals covered the territory to the southward, and we are told that a total of no less than 660,000 acres, or more than 1000 square miles, was served by this project. With the passage of time the river has cut down its bed and built up the plain until at present the old Han intake, which may still be identified, is more than forty feet above the bed of the stream. As nature made it increasingly difficult to get water from the river onto the land, the intake for the main canal was moved farther and farther up the narrow gorge. Its construction, in the solid rock along the side of the cliff, must have been a tremendous task, considering the implements employed. This mammoth work, once so beneficial, is now practically useless, for the limit of the native Chinese methods has been reached. Only six thousand acres, or less than ten square miles, is now watered by the project.

Benefits from Irrigation of the Shensi Plain

The Wei-pei plain is the richest grain-growing area in Shensi province. In good years it not only furnishes food for the surrounding territory but helps also to feed the people of southern Shansi and western Honan. But it is, unfortunately, one of the driest regions in this section of China, and only occasionally are bumper crops harvested; every few years they are a total failure. The Famine Commission, after having spent more than a million dollars in Shensi for relief work in 1920–1921, half as much again in Shansi, and nearly four times that amount in Honan, felt that the time had arrived to investigate the possibilities of doing

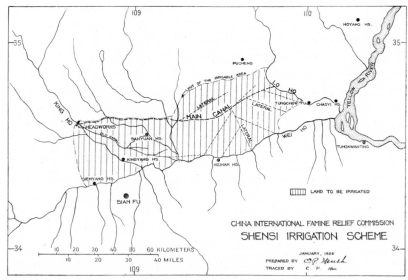

FIG. 82—The Wei Ho valley is the richest grain-growing area of Shensi but is subject to frequent drought.

something to prevent, if possible, the early repetition of such conditions. The old irrigation scheme was examined, and a staff of modern-trained engineers was engaged to make a thorough survey of the region. The result of this study is a project, whose details are now being worked out, that will provide water for an area of 680,000 acres, or more than was provided for by the original scheme at the time of its greatest efficiency. The plan includes the construction of a high concrete dam far up the gorge of the King River and a tunnel more than a mile and a half long through a mountain, neither of which features could be accomplished by native methods. The estimated cost of the first section of the scheme is approximately $1,500,000, Chinese currency. This will provide water for more than a third of the area.

The benefits of this work from the point of view of famine prevention alone will be enormous. The present average crop on nonirrigated land is probably about 800 pounds an acre, while on the small section that is watered the yield is three times as great, or 2400 pounds an acre. Thus the provision of sufficient moisture would increase the grain supply of the province by more than a billion pounds annually, and this is enough to feed a population of more than two million people, according to the diet outlined in the first chapter. In addition to the increase in crops and because of this increase, the value of property would be considerably enhanced. The present cost of nonirrigated land on the plain is estimated at $60, Chinese currency, an acre; but of irrigated land, from $120 to $180. At an average of $150 an acre, the increased value of the lands in the province resulting from the construction of this work will be more than $60,000,-000, while the total cost of the whole scheme will be but a small fraction of this sum.

Irrigation on the Great Plains

In the plains far removed from the hills, where the need is equally great, the problem is more difficult of solution. It is a pitiable sight to see the crops along the course of the Yellow River in Honan and Shantung dried to a cinder for want of moisture, while just a few feet away on the other side of the dike is water in abundance. A careful survey of the plains would probably reveal many localities where water released from the rivers would, if properly led, spread over large areas by gravity alone. This subject is worthy of detailed technical study.

On account of the danger of breaking the dikes, even if provided with proper gates, it would perhaps be most satisfactory to take water over them by siphon. For it must be remembered that the rivers are in many cases higher than the surrounding country—which makes the siphon method possible—and in almost every instance are held in their courses solely by means of earthen dikes. Without accurate maps, which at present are few and confined to a small section of the country, it is not possible to estimate how far this idea could be developed. The writer, from his travels back and forth across the plains, is inclined to believe that very wide areas could be irrigated by this means along the lower courses of many of the larger rivers. The points for taking water from the streams would need to be selected with care, for they should provide sufficient fall and should be situated where the course of the river is stable, particularly during the low-water season. It must be borne in mind also that the irrigation canals would silt up rather quickly, particularly with Yellow River or Yung Ting River water. Hence, considerable upkeep work would be necessary. But, knowing the benefits of a dependable water supply, the farmers, if properly directed, could be induced to do this work in the spare time at their disposal, or a water tax could be imposed to provide funds for it.

The losses from a flood are recompensed, to a degree, by the enrichment of the soil resulting from a deposition of new earth from the flood waters. Irrigation effects this improvement without the accompanying losses, and its benefits are therefore twofold.

Irrigation from Wells and Reservoirs

Irrigation from wells is a practice widely followed, the water being raised either by human labor or by that of animals. The writer has never seen power-driven pumps in China, and probably, considering the abundance of labor, they would be profitable only in large enterprises where the benefits and the costs might be shared by a whole community. But while irrigation from wells is widely known and has been practiced for centuries, it is capable of great expansion. A geological survey would reveal districts where water is obtainable although undiscovered by the residents. In other districts farmers are aware that there is water but have not the means or enterprise to sink their wells to a sufficient depth. In 1920–1921 the Famine Commission and the American Red Cross invested nearly $200,000, Chinese currency, in digging wells, more than six thousand of them, for irrigation purposes. The increase in value of one crop alone was more than enough to repay the cost of the work. Each well provides water for four acres, on the average, so that this undertaking assures a dependable yield to 24,000 acres. If we estimate the increase which results from this improvement on the same basis as for the Wei-pei scheme, the total annual increase of grain would amount to more than 25,000,000 pounds, or food enough for fifty thousand people. These figures are not, of course, exact. There are many local factors which might change them considerably either way, but they indicate in general what enormous improvements can be effected in this backward country with the introduction of new ideas or the extension of old ones.

It is customary in some districts, particularly in central China, to store water in the rainy season which may later be used for irrigation and other purposes. Huge tanks or reservoirs are built in the ground from which the water is led or pumped onto the fields in the dry season. The practice is not at all general and is capable of great extension and improvement. The reservoirs silt up year by year until they often become too shallow to hold sufficient water for the season. This, of course, is particularly the case in years of drought. By a better organization of the villagers the tanks could be deepened and enlarged during the slack season of the year when the population is practically idle. A good deal of labor would be involved, for the capacity of the reservoirs is dependent on depth rather than breadth, since it is not economically sound to take too large an area out of cultivation.

Irrigation from wells provides a good crop in normal years and in years when the rainfall alone is not quite sufficient. But when prolonged droughts occur, the limitations of this method become apparent, for the wells run dry. The situation is even worse with storage cisterns for rain water, for these give out first of all.

Cures for Flood Famine: Tree Planting in Foothills and Gullies

It is generally believed that floods are preventable, and vast sums of money have been spent, not only in China but also in the West, in the effort to control the watercourses. In China, the work has been based on empirical rather than scientific knowledge. Dikes have been built without accurate surveys and with little reference to the laws of hydraulics. Even in the West, where scientific principles have been employed and flood-prevention works are of more permanent construction, the problem has not been completely solved. In 1925, for instance, severe inundations occurred in several countries in Europe because the dikes did not hold. Modern engineering practices, however, have prevented a great many disasters which could not have been avoided by the old methods. Only in a limited number of places in China have such practices been applied. In fact, only a few of China's rivers have even been surveyed by modern methods.

If all silt could be eliminated from the streams and if the run-off from heavy rainfall could be retarded in the hills instead of immediately rushing down the steep slopes into the rivers, the problem of preventing severe floods would be a comparatively easy one. Foresters tell us that the planting of trees in the hill country will accomplish these results, for a thick forest cover will break the force of a heavy rainstorm and the layer of leaves and the network of roots will prevent the washing away of the soil. The water will filter slowly through the humus, reaching the rivers in the plains below in smaller volume, and extending its beneficent effects over a longer time. While it is almost impossible to plant trees on the higher slopes it can be done along the lower gullies near the streams and so help to hold up the soil washed down from above and also do something toward retarding the rate of run-off. This is the method advocated by W. C. Lowdermilk of the College of Agriculture and Forestry, Nanking University.[35]

[35] W. C. Lowdermilk: Erosion and Floods in the Yellow River Watershed. *Journ. of Forestry*, Vol. 22, 1924, pp. 11–18.

FIG. 83

FIG. 84

FIG. 83—A layer of coarse sand left by the floods ruined this good farm land.
FIG. 84—One beneficial effect of the floods is the layer of rich silt sometimes
left on the fields.

Engineering Projects Also Needed

But the forester's ideal will never be reached; and, while he is doing what he can to bring about fundamental changes, it will be necessary to call upon the engineer to undertake those more temporary, but none the less important, improvements along the lower courses of the rivers, supplemented perhaps by the construction of detention reservoirs in the hills by which the rate of flow may be artificially controlled.

The amount of soil that a stream can hold in suspension and carry to the sea is related to the velocity of the current and the depth of the water,—both of which factors can be regulated through modern engineering methods by the straightening of channels and the construction of strong, well-protected dikes. The tremendous losses described in the second chapter as resulting from the frequent overflow of the Hwai River in Kiangsu Province can be prevented by the construction of a suitable outlet to carry these heavy floods to the sea. A complete and authoritative survey has never been made of the whole region involved; but the Famine Commission, through its Shanghai Committee, has been working towards this end, and a final investigation will be made and a specific scheme adopted as soon as political conditions permit.

The Hwai River Conservancy

Although a definite project has not been decided upon, certain proposals have been made by eminent engineers, and rough estimates of the necessary outlay have been prepared. Three plans have been presented, of which that of the American hydraulic engineer, Mr. John R. Freeman, is the most favored because it appears to be the cheapest. The other two were drawn up by the board of engineers of the American Red Cross in 1914 and by the Chinese National Conservancy Bureau respectively.

Mr. Freeman's proposal, which is for the construction of a straight channel from Hungtze Lake to the sea, would probably cost about $12,000,000, Chinese currency. The

American Red Cross project, which would take off the flood waters of the Hwai through increasing the capacity of the Grand Canal, is estimated at $60,000,000, while the Chinese plan, which provides not only for the improvement of the Grand Canal but also for a channel in the old bed of the Yellow River and very comprehensive improvement to the upper course of the Hwai River, is calculated to require $213,000,000.

For purposes of famine prevention the Freeman scheme is the best, for the first requisite is to provide as soon as possible an outlet to the sea for the flood waters. The other plans carry refinements which, while of great economic benefit, should not be permitted to block the commencement of the work by the difficulty of raising the larger sums required. Also the time needed for the installation of the various schemes is a matter to be considered, that of the Red Cross engineers requiring six years while that of the Conservancy Board is estimated to require ten years. The Freeman plan provides for the immediate digging of the outlet channel; and any refinements for improving navigation, providing water for irrigation, etc., are to be added later when the danger of serious inundation is less acute.

It has already been stated that the frequent floods of this river cause a loss of food sufficient to provide for a population of more than 7,000,000 people. If a comprehensive project is carried out, this loss will be prevented. In addition, an area of 700,000 acres of submerged land in the lakes will be reclaimed by the Freeman project; and this will feed an additional 3,500,000 people, assuming the yield to be 2000 pounds an acre. There would also be a considerable economic gain from the improvement in navigation that would be made in the Grand Canal and from the provision of water for irrigation of the area between the Grand Canal and the sea. According to the estimate of an expert of the Commission for the Readjustment of Finance, in an article on this subject printed in the Chinese Economic Monthly, the economic gain would total more than a billion dollars a year, Chinese currency.[36] This is made up as follows:

[36] *Chinese Econ. Monthly*, Vol. 2, No. 15, Chinese Govt. Bur. of Econ. Information, Peking.

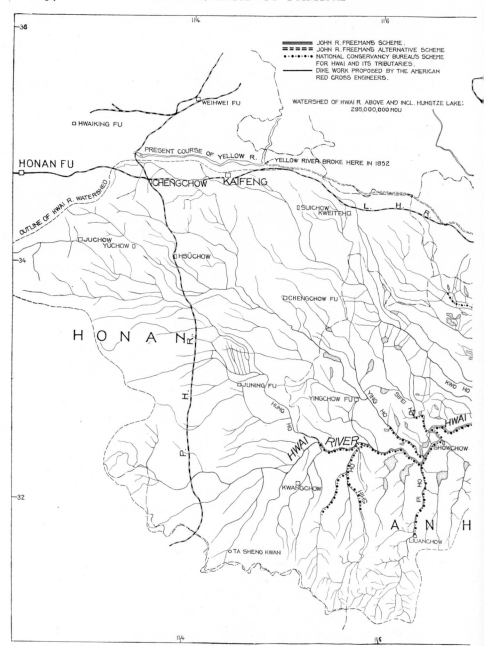

FIG. 85—Various conservancy schemes for the Hwai River, provinces of Anhwei and Kiangsu. Scale 1 : 3,500,000.

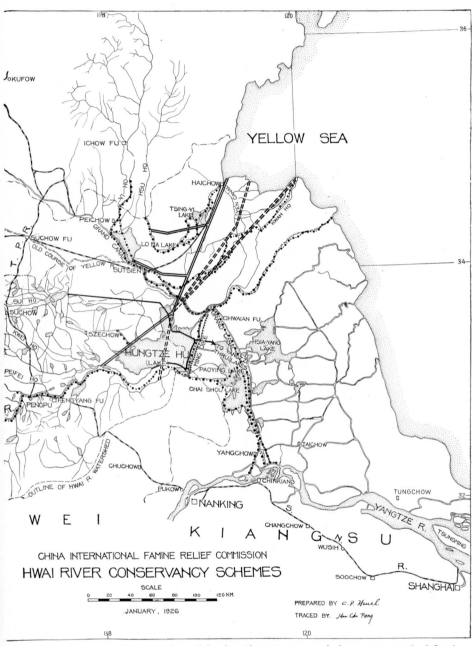

YELLOW SEA

CHINA INTERNATIONAL FAMINE RELIEF COMMISSION
HWAI RIVER CONSERVANCY SCHEMES

SCALE
0 20 40 60 80 100 120 KM

JANUARY, 1926

PREPARED BY C.P. Heuel
TRACED BY Han Chi Peng

From the point of view of famine distress no area is in greater need of flood prevention.

Gain from land subject to flood, estimated at 10,500,000
    acres (land inundated in 1921), at $60 an acre $630,000,000
Yield on 1,250,000 acres to be reclaimed, at $60 an acre .   75,000,000
Improvement to 33,333,333 acres at $12 an acre   400,000,000

                                                  $1,105,000,000

This is computed on the complete scheme proposed by the Chinese National Conservancy Bureau.

THE YELLOW RIVER

The fact that the Yellow River has made but three considerable changes in its course in the past thousand years is an indication that a large measure of control of this difficult stream has been obtained by native methods. It is astonishing that without any accurate knowledge of the elevation of the country, in fact, without even the instruments for acquiring such information, dikes could be constructed that have endured for many hundreds of years. Not only have earthern dikes been built, but they have been reënforced by stone; while in many critical places protective groins have been constructed to deflect the swift current from the dikes.

Modern engineering methods, however, can make the river even more safe, and the following passage from a report of Engineer Freeman's should assist in dispelling any doubt as to their efficacy:

The result of all information that the writer has been able to obtain about the elevation of the Yellow River's flood waters above that of the plain outside the dikes, together with his personal inspection while floating down along the stream in December, 1919, have convinced him that the river is no such fierce and ungovernable tyrant as it has been painted, and that it regularly carries to the sea more than 99 per cent of the sediment which it digs and brings down over the vast loess deposits upstream from the apex of the delta, that the rate of raising its bed after having reached its present elevation is hardly more than one foot in a hundred years, and that means for confining the channel in a straight and narrow way and forcing it to dig its bed deeper are within economic reach, and as to the many outbreaks recorded in history and shown by the looped dikes on the reconnaissance maps, it is plain that these are the result of human carelessness and official negligence rather than the result of the wrath of the river gods.

FIG. 86

FIG. 87

FIG. 88

FIG. 86—A new Famine Commission dike on the Yangtze River.

FIG. 87—Land reclaimed from the Yangtze River by a dike project of the Famine Commission.

FIG. 88—A completed Famine Commission stone-faced dike.

The Yellow River in its upper reaches is well confined in its course by hills, and not until it emerges onto the great plain in the western part of Honan province does the danger begin. From here to the sea, a distance of approximately 500 miles, there are dikes on both sides; but these dikes follow the course of the stream in all its meanderings instead of confining it in a straight channel. The low-water surface is on the average fifteen feet above the general level of the plain outside the main dikes, while in the high-water season the surface rises to thirty feet above the plain. The dikes are nominally five feet higher still but in many places are not adequately maintained at that height.

The Famine Commission has begun a thorough survey of the course of the river under the management of its chief engineer, Mr. O. J. Todd, who has had a wider experience with this stream than has any other foreign expert. Since 1920 he has constructed many miles of dikes along its banks, and in 1923 he designed and carried to completion the reversion works at Liching in Shantung—a project similar to but more difficult than the well-known control works of the lower Colorado River in America. A considerable stretch in western Honan has already been mapped. The Commission proposes to adopt a comprehensive scheme for the permanent control of the river and in case of future famines in Honan and Shantung to utilize relief funds in paying able-bodied members of refugee families to work on the project, beginning at the western end.

No estimate of the total cost of this work can be definitely made until the surveys are complete. The work can be done in sections beginning at the upstream end. The constriction of the stream also will reclaim large stretches of land. Probably this reclaimed and very rich land will be valuable enough to pay for a large part of the cost of the work, for in some places the dikes are many miles apart. If this territory were sold as it is redeemed and the proceeds used for construction of the next section, the work, after it was once started, would be almost self-supporting.

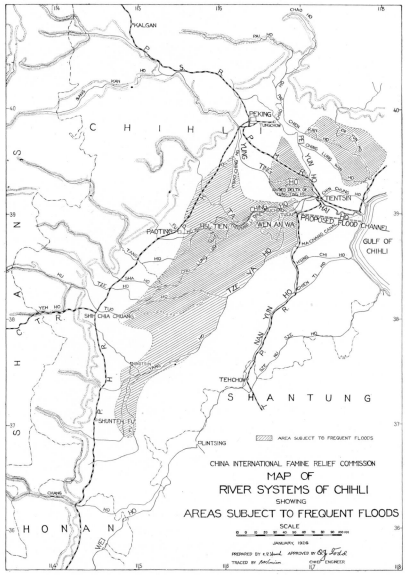

FIG. 89—It is proposed to solve the flood problem in Chihli by a flood channel to supplement drainage via the Hai Ho. Scale of map 1 : 4,000,000.

No statistical estimate can be made of the benefits to be derived from the improvement of the Yellow River, for there is no particular flood area that is inundated at regular intervals. However, permanent control would protect Shantung and Honan provinces from the danger of flood for many years to come, and the increased production of foodstuffs on the reclaimed land would greatly help to prevent famines.

Flood Prevention in Chihli

The disastrous floods occurring every few years in Chihli are preventable and present a much simpler and less expensive problem than the control of either the Hwai or Yellow Rivers. The solution, we are told by engineers, is to provide an additional channel to the sea from the main ponding area. This will serve to supplement the Hai Ho, which is now the only outlet for the flow of several rivers converging at the city of Tientsin. This channel would be about 45 miles in length, 450 feet wide, and 12 feet deep. It would carry twice the quantity of water discharged by the Hai Ho at its maximum flow; and the cost for earthwork, according to the Famine Commission's estimates, would be about $6,000,000, Chinese currency, if done with famine labor. Even an elaborate project, to include refinements in addition to the simple construction of the flood channel, it is estimated would call for only $12,000,000, and this is but 16 per cent of the calculated loss from the last flood.

The benefits of this project, in addition to rendering Tientsin, the largest port in northern China, safe from inundation, would be the provision of crop insurance for an area of approximately ten thousand square miles of the richest farm land in the province—an area nearly as great as that of Belgium.

Similar proposals are applicable to many rivers, the more important ones being the Pearl and the Yangtze. On these and other rivers such improvements could be carried out as have been demonstrated in other countries to be thoroughly effective. The costs would be heavy but light in comparison with the benefits derived, and there would be little danger of failure if proper technical supervision were given.

LAND RECLAMATION

The failure of dikes in past ages or changes in the courses of the rivers has inundated large areas in China, and neglect to make proper repairs has in some cases resulted in the formation of permanent lakes. In many instances the water that has taken this land out of production does not reach any considerable depth, and the draining of these inland seas, or the reclamation by diking of a part of the area now flooded, is not an insuperable task. The proper improvement of the Yangtze River and its tributaries will redeem large tracts now forming the beds of Tungting and Poyang Lakes. The Hwai conservancy scheme will at least partially drain the Hungtze and several other lakes in Kiangsu province whose combined area is more than 1800 square miles; and there are other projects of less importance, whose completion would be proportionately beneficial.

THE LOCUST PROBLEM

A world-wide effort is being put forth to solve the locust problem; experiments are being conducted in various countries, including a study of the possibility of introducing parasites to the insects, an investigation of the effectiveness of spraying swarms from airplanes, as well as a consideration of the industrial uses to which the dead insects could be put. If useful products could be made from the carcasses of locusts so that they had a commercial value, a method of killing the insects would speedily be found. Another constructive proposal for meeting catastrophes wrought by these pests is an insurance project advocated in Europe—the farmers of all countries taking out policies, whose premiums would serve to indemnify individuals in blighted areas.

Locust insurance might be undertaken in China with beneficial results if honestly directed, but it is unlikely that enough farmers would avail themselves of it to make it effective in preventing famine distress after a severe visitation. There are in most families no extra funds even in normal years, for a good crop means only a better diet and not ready money. Hence it would be almost impossible, especially for the poorer people, to find funds to pay the premium.

At the Pan-Pacific Food Conservation Conference held at Honolulu in the summer of 1924, the following resolution was passed:

Whereas, in all Pacific countries that are subject to plagues of locusts or grasshoppers, it is highly advisable that accurate scientific surveys be made of lands which may constitute the permanent breeding grounds of these insects; and that, when such permanent breeding grounds are delimited with some degree of certainty, it is important that they be scouted at frequent intervals in order to learn the prospects concerning approaching devastating flights, and in order to begin preventive measures at the earliest moment.

Resolved, That the governments of the Pacific countries be advised to make such surveys and to establish, where possible, in permanent breeding regions biological stations for the study of the factors in natural control.

Resolved further, That where swarms originating from definitely located permanent breeding areas, customarily enter lands controlled by different governments such governments are urged to establish and to defray the expenses of cooperative commissions charged with the promotion of such procedures as are indicated in the preceding resolution.[37]

There is great need for a biological study of this pest by some international organization having facilities for making the necessary observations in all countries. These studies should then be followed by the formulation of a plan of attack to be undertaken simultaneously by the various countries of the world. Unless treated in some such comprehensive fashion there is little hope for success in eradicating this scourge.

For other natural calamities that may occasionally produce local famine distress, such as earthquakes, typhoons, hailstorms, and frost, there is no known cure. Crops may in some instances be covered to protect them from hail and frost; and, when severe storms occur on coasts, stronger sea walls may serve to keep back the salt water from ruining farm land.

[37] *Proc. First Pan-Pacific Food Conservation Conf.*, Honolulu, 1925, p. 185.

FIG. 90—The Great Wall at Kupehkow. (Photograph by F. G. Clapp.)

CHAPTER VII

POLITICAL CURES FOR FAMINE

China is at present engaged in a great experiment. She has no traditions on which to build a truly representative government, and, considering the lack of education and the backwardness and poverty of the masses, it is a question if such a government can be evolved without the disintegration of the territory now comprising the republic or the assumption of the reins of power by some despot able to exact obedience. China is really today a republic only in name. There has never been an election, and the control of the state has been effected by the display of force rather than by the will of the citizens.

There are some who ascribe all the ills manifested by the new régime to the last dynasty, asserting that these are inherited disabilities of the decadent Manchu house. But, even assuming that this is true, it does not explain how these evils are to be eradicated, how dishonest officials are to become public-spirited, how the fatalistic philosophy of the race is to be replaced by a sense of civic responsibility, how the present reign of force is to be exchanged for a reign of law and the war lords induced to disband their armies and turn over the administration of the country to civil authorities. Time alone will tell—probably a considerable lapse of time—how this can be accomplished; and it is the writer's opinion that if and when an effective and stable central government is evolved, it will conform much more closely to the requirements of Chinese political philosophy than the Western-made republican model so hastily adopted.

Form of Government Not Important

But for the creation of conditions that will result in the prevention of famines it makes little difference what precise form the government takes so long as it is maintained in the interests of the people rather than for the personal profit of the officials. Confucius said: "The requisites of government are that there be sufficiency of food, sufficiency of military equipment, and the confidence of the people in their ruler." When asked which of these was least important, he said: "The military equipment"; and when questioned as to which of the two remaining might be dispensed with first, he said: "Part with the food. From of old, death has been the lot of all men; but if the people have no faith in their rulers, there is no standing for the state."

Stable Government Would Stop Losses from War

The first beneficial effects that would result from the establishment of a stable and effective government would be a cessation of the evils of civil war, which have been discussed in Chapter III. One of the first steps would be the suppression of banditry and the disbandment of superfluous troops. Disbandment involves more than a million men, if we assume that a standing army of 500,000 is enough to maintain order and protect from foreign invasion. This is roughly four times the peace strength of the standing army of the United States, which has only a fourth of China's population. There has been much talk of the disbandment of the mercenaries with which the various military leaders have surrounded themselves and by which they maintain their positions; but the problem is a larger one than at first appears. Not only must the chieftains agree to relinquish their power, but some provision must be made for properly disarming and disbanding their troops and getting them back to their homes or finding them employment. For a coolie to find work in a district to which he is a stranger is almost impossible. Many interesting proposals have been put forward for the employment of disbanded troops on con-

Fig. 91

Fig. 92

Fig. 93

Fig. 91—The Chinese sawmill.   Labor is plentiful and cheap.

Fig. 92—Reeds in the Chihli lake region are used to make mats.

Fig. 93—The Famine Commission mat-making project employed flood victims in their homes.

servancy schemes; this is an excellent idea, but first there must be political stability so that funds for the construction of such projects may be forthcoming.

Reduction in the annual government expenditure for war purposes would make it possible either to lower taxes or to undertake constructive enterprises. This assumes, of course, that demilitarization is accomplished by a reputable government and honest officials.

PRESENT OFFICIAL VIEW ON FAMINE PREVENTION

A striking example of the present view of the military leaders on the problem of famine prevention was afforded the writer in an interview with Marshal Wu Pei-fu several years ago when he was virtually the dictator of the Chinese government. The purpose of the conversation was to discuss ways and means for the control of the Yellow River in Honan province. The Famine Commission was prepared to start its survey of the country through which the stream flows and sought government approval and coöperation. The Marshal showed much interest in the matter, but it was difficult to convince him that a careful survey should be made. "Why go to the expense of making surveys"? he said, "I have a perfectly good military map which shows the course of the river, which I shall be glad to give you." Upon being assured that a survey would be necessary and that the Commission was prepared to defray the cost he reluctantly consented.

In the course of an hour's discussion it became evident that General Wu had ideas of his own on the subject of river control. He first explained that the great difficulty was the quantity of silt carried down from the hills and deposited in the stream bed every year. If that silt could be kept in suspension it would be carried to the sea and the problem would be solved. He proposed the purchase of a number of tug boats to which could be attached a large spiked anchor much like a chestnut burr. He thought that if there were a number of these tugs steaming up and down the river dragging their spiked anchors, the silt would be stirred up and carried to the ocean several hundred miles downstream.

As we were about to leave, the Marshal mentioned the subject of roads of which the Commission had built some hundreds of miles not far from his headquarters. "Your roads are much too narrow" he said, "only twenty feet where they should be sixty." I explained that if a twenty-foot road were built three times the mileage could be constructed with a given sum of money. But he was quite firm in his opinion. "All my roads are sixty feet wide," he insisted; and there the matter ended. It is true that he did build some roads sixty feet wide, using his troops for the work, but a road of such width is of no greater service than a twenty-foot road except, perhaps, for troop movements. This all goes to show that Wu Pei-fu's main energy and thought were directed to military rather than civil affairs; for he is a man of education, and, if really interested, would inform himself on matters so important to China as river conservancy and road building.

But, while cessation of civil strife would prevent great losses, it is the constructive side of the problem that would effect the greatest insurance against starvation conditions among the people.

CROP ESTIMATES AND RESERVES OF GRAIN

Most famines, particularly those due to drought, can be anticipated if there is a proper crop-reporting system. Crop estimates can be made at fixed times through the growing season, and a sufficiently accurate appraisal of the situation arrived at to forecast the probable yield over the whole country. If such information were collected by the county officials in China and forwarded promptly to the central government, plans to meet any impending distress in the regions where crop failure was threatened could be drawn up well in advance. Although some data are collected, the present system is entirely unsatisfactory, because the information is not put into usable form until months after the crops have actually been harvested. Poor communications with interior districts and civil strife tend to make further delays. An efficient and reliable crop-reporting section of, say, the Government Bureau of Economic Information is a vital part of a famine-relief or famine-prevention bureau.

The collection of reserves of grain in the walled cities throughout the provinces subject to famine distress should be encouraged. This grain need not be given to the people in the form of doles, in fact, it should not be so distributed excepting in emergencies; but it should be put on the market at cost to prevent hoarding and profiteering during periods of shortage. It should also be used by the government to recompense laborers engaged during famine times on the construction of public utilities.

NEED OF GOVERNMENT SUPPORT FOR BETTER LAND UTILIZATION

We hear a great deal about the conservatism of the Chinese farmers, but, given the means to effect improvements and having concrete proof that these means will bring the desired results, the Chinese will adopt new methods. The government should provide the means and should undertake the demonstration of the beneficial effect of more scientific procedure in raising foodstuffs. It is impossible to state just what sum is devoted to the maintenance of the Agricultural Department of the government. It is perfectly safe, however, to say that expenditures are entirely inadequate to bring about the improvements that would serve to raise the standard of living of the farming population.

Government action is especially needed for afforestation and forest protection. On a visit to the Western Tombs, where many of the emperors of the last dynasty are buried, the writer witnessed the wholesale destruction of the forests now taking place. This is one of the few places in China proper where even a semblance of a forest exists. The old trees have been preserved for hundreds of years, but the

FIG. 94

FIG. 95

FIG. 94—The beautiful old trees at the Western Tombs are now being cut down by the troops.   (Photograph by T. J. Betts.)

FIG. 95—There are literally millions of acres where valuable forests would grow.

military authorities are now systematically cutting them
down to sell for lumber and to use for fuel. We inquired of
some of the troops why this was being done and were told
that the regiment billeted there was a "forestry" regiment.
Its duty was to protect and preserve the trees; but, since
they were now no longer the property of the Manchus but
belonged to the "people," they, as the people's representa-
tives, were cutting some of them down and shipping them to
the railhead to be sold. This was said to be necessary in
order that funds might be provided for the regular payment
of the "forestry" regiment.

About ten years ago a Forest Service was organized by the
government as a Department of the Ministry of Agriculture
and Commerce. According to Mr. Dau-yang Lin, $181,000,
Mexican currency, was appropriated as its first year's
budget.[38] The number of men engaged in China's forest
service totaled only 70. Germany with an area only about one-
twentieth as great employed more than 9000, and in Russia
a force of 36,000 was maintained before the Great War. Mr.
Lin also compares the relative expenditures of the nations
for maintenance for a forest service and shows that China's
$181,000 is only about a two-hundred-and-fiftieth of Ger-
many's budget and a fiftieth of America's.

In connection with the utilization of the land, reference
must again be made to the growth of the opium poppy,
which takes good grain land out of cultivation. Less than
ten years ago the cultivation of the poppy was almost entirely
stopped, but with the continuance of civil commotion the
acreage has increased year after year until now it is as widely
grown as ever. A stable government could successfully
solve this great problem, which has such an important effect
on the well-being of the masses.

CHINESE BUSINESS ON SOUND BASIS

One of the enigmas of present-day China is the apparent
ability of the people to pursue a "business-as-usual" course
in spite of the absolute political chaos with which they are

[38] Dau-yang Lin: Chapters on China and Forestry, Shanghai, 1916.

surrounded. The Maritime Customs returns show a constantly increasing volume of foreign trade, factories are being built, new industries introduced, markets for new products opened up, and a slow but steady advance made year by year in the modernization of the country. Last year, amid frequent changes in government, student riots, and civil wars around the capital, a street railway was opened in Peking for the first time in her history; and, in spite of frequent difficulties with troops who insist on riding free and in spite of coal famines due to the interruption of railway communications, the street cars still run and, we must assume, make a profit. Another instance of business progress is given by the U. S. Department of Commerce:

> There is no more striking example of China's ability to progress in the face of what appears to be insurmountable obstacles than the developments in the past few years in Canton. The contrast between the Canton of to-day and of seven years ago is striking enough when it is considered that this remarkable development took place within the remarkably short space of seven years, but it is even more startling when it is understood that these seven years represented the most stormy period of Canton's history—years of civil war and strife, extending from the city itself to all parts of the neighboring provinces.[39]

Such facts show the soundness of the Chinese business fabric. With this background the tremendous possibilities for the industrial development of the country, if given proper government, can be estimated.

Famine Relief Methods

The China International Famine Relief Commission during this interim of governmental impotence is doing all that an organization inspired by philanthropic motives and carried on as a purely nongovernmental agency can hope to do. Its greatest contribution to the famine question has been the working out of a method of treatment that in many respects is novel and which may later be taken over by the authorities. This method, as will be explained later, uses the

[39] J. H. Nelson: Changing Factors in the Economic Life of China, *U. S. Dept. of Commerce, Trade Information Bull. No. 312, 1925.*

funds contributed for famine relief in such a way as to leave, after the emergency is past, permanent works of a famine-prevention character. A somewhat similar policy has been adopted by the Indian government. The Famine Commission, it may be noted, worked out its program quite independently; and not until its policy had been completely formed did it discover that practices in India were in some respects almost identical.

The Chinese government method of distributing relief funds in times of disaster is not unlike the practices followed by governments the world over where public money is divided among the people. It is customary in such instances to make an even distribution among the sufferers, and, since the funds are usually too meager to provide adequately for all the needy until the following harvest, the sufferers receive only enough to prolong life for a few days, after which they die and the relief funds are buried with them. Philanthropic societies in China, following the government's lead, have adopted much the same practice; but some of them have gone a step further and selected a smaller number of beneficiaries providing sufficient relief to keep them alive until they can reap a harvest or by some other means regain their self-support. In both of these instances, however, the people are supported in idleness; for both flood and drought result in a destruction of the crops, leaving nothing for the rural population to do until the next planting season. This has a distinctly unfavorable effect on the farmers and tends to lower their morale and force self-respecting country folk into the pauper class.

The American Red Cross in its China Famine Relief Work in 1920–1921 adopted the plan of furnishing employment to the able-bodied members of stricken families.[40] In return for a day's labor on some public work sufficient relief was provided to support the laborer and his dependents. The wages paid were on a piece-work basis and were intentionally kept below the normal wage scale in order that only the

[40] Report of the China Famine Relief, American Red Cross, October, 1920–September, 1921, Shanghai.

FIG. 96

FIG. 97

FIG. 98

FIG. 96—The Famine Commission gives relief in return for labor on famine-prevention works. A Han River dike project.

FIG. 97—Flood-prevention work in Hupeh province built with famine labor.

FIG. 98—A Famine Commission dike project in Kiangsi province.

actually needy might be assisted. Thus the professional mendicants were automatically eliminated, as no one who could possibly get along otherwise would toil for less than the usual rate of pay. Failure to find in any region persons who were willing to work under these conditions proved that the particular region was not seriously affected. This Red Cross experiment was not the first of its kind in China, but it was the first of any importance. The work accomplished was the construction of roads, of which 850 miles were built during the emergency.

At the close of the Red Cross operations a large part of the public were still unconvinced of the superior advantages of the labor relief plan. Hence when the Famine Commission announced that it would adopt this policy so far as possible for all its operations there was opposition in some quarters. However, after six years' continuous experience of the benefits of such a course nearly all its opponents have been won over. The Famine Commission has greatly developed the Red Cross scheme. Now the policy of employing the able-bodied victims of a disaster is not followed for social considerations alone but for economic reasons as well. Projects having a distinct famine-prevention angle are now selected, such as irrigation, flood-prevention, and land reclamation. In places where there are no undertakings that contribute to the increase of production or the conservation of foodstuffs, road building is chosen, opportunity for which is always and everywhere available in China.

A REVOLVING FUND FOR FAMINE-PREVENTION PROJECTS

Since projects of the sort mentioned above are revenue-producing or revenue-conserving, a further feature has recently been added. It is now the Commission's practice, wherever possible, to regard sums expended on such works as a loan to the community benefited and to expect a return as soon as practicable, whereupon the funds are devoted to other areas needing assistance. A nominal interest charge is made to cover administrative and engineering costs.

It will thus be seen that the Commission affords a means of organization and finance that has hitherto been lacking in rural China. For instance, a flood occurs in a certain province, rendering the people destitute. In order to save the population the Famine Commission agrees to loan a million dollars. This money is expended by the Commission's agents in repairing the dike system, the failure of which caused the inundation. The otherwise idle villagers are recruited to do the work, and the wage they receive, which is less than the normal scale, keeps them alive. With the dikes restored and the danger of flood removed a good crop is harvested, and ample funds are available to reimburse the Commission so that similar emergencies can be met in other places. Or perhaps a famine occurs from drought. The relief funds are used to construct a large irrigation scheme, the work being done by the victims of the disaster. The provision of a dependable water supply makes good crops possible, and the return of the funds is made by a contribution from the farmers whose land is served. In both cases the food supply is increased, and future famines to a considerable extent are obviated.

Quite apart from the usefulness of this work in itself, its greatest benefit is the lesson taught. What tremendous good would accrue, and what a great step would be taken toward relieving China's 400,000,000 people from the constant threat of famine, if a stable government with adequate funds were to assume responsibility for carrying through to its logical conclusion the undertaking already started! For it has been proved to be thoroughly sound.

Government Famine Bureau

As soon as an effective government is formed, the writer would propose the establishment of a Famine Prevention Bureau directly under the Cabinet Office, which should be charged also with the government relief work. This bureau to be effective must be granted extensive powers and be organized for works of widely diversified character. Many elements must be treated simultaneously to bring the most salutary results. There must be close coöperation with the regular government departments, especially the Ministry of Agriculture and Commerce, the Ministry of Communications, and the Ministry of Education. It is for these reasons that a special bureau is recommended, and it should be placed under the Cabinet Office to give it independence and authority.

While the National Famine Prevention Bureau should be established by the central government, its operations should be made effective through similar departments of the provincial administrations. The provincial bureaus would be responsible for carrying out the actual work of relief, reporting regularly to the central office. Authority to remit taxes, both national and provincial, should be vested in this department.

There should be maintained an executive organization capable of rapid expansion in emergencies and including the necessary technical staff and equipment. In the interim between famines it should devote itself to laying plans and preparing projects against future disasters.

The above may be regarded as the relief functions of the bureau. More important than these is the preventive work. Conservancy, irrigation, land-reclamation, and flood-control works should be undertaken as the necessary funds are provided by the government, and the same organization and staff that function during a famine can be thus employed between periods of disaster. Following the plan of the American Reclamation Bureau or the Famine Commission, these projects can be carried out on a revolving fund basis, for the benefits will be many times greater than the cost in all cases where the schemes are practical. The Government Famine Bureau would have a great advantage over the Famine Commission in that it could collect repayment for works constructed by a tax on those who benefited by them. This the Commission, as an unofficial body, is, of course, unable to do. It has had little difficulty, however, in collecting its loans.

Coöperation with other Departments

This bureau should effect a liaison with the proposed crop-reporting sections of the Bureau of Economic Information. In this way a shortage of food in any area could be foretold before famine conditions are actually upon the people. There are other signs than crops indicating imminence of famine distress—influx of beggars into the towns and cities; rapid rise in the price of foodstuffs and in the interest rate; unusual wandering of people, to be marked especially along the railways. Local officials should be instructed to report such conditions to the bureau, as well as to give prompt and complete data on any natural disaster, such as flood or the visitation of locusts.

Assuming that the policy of giving relief in return for labor is adopted by the government, it will be seen that a close coöperation must be maintained between the bureau and the Public Works Department of the various provinces. The writer would propose that all conservancy work that would normally be undertaken by the central government should be put under the bureau. If this were done, projects of predetermined benefit could be prepared in advance in almost all districts. Close contact with the Ministry of Communications would make it possible to employ large numbers of able-bodied victims on road and railway construction, and the portions of such projects requiring manual labor should be pushed forward with vigor during famine periods.

Other Famine Prevention Work

While conservancy work is being carried out by one division of the bureau, other divisions should be formed to effect crop improvements, to promote forestry, to develop and stimulate rural industries, and to introduce better credit facilities for the country population. A close liaison should be established with the Ministry of Education in order that the bureau's influence may be brought to bear on the educational policies, particularly those of the country and the agricultural schools.

Above all, the appalling results which a continuance of present conditions will inevitably produce must be brought home to the people of China, and the possibilities of improvement must be discovered and strongly advocated. This can most effectively be done by a properly managed government department. Famines, which have long been recognized as nature's ruthless means of keeping down the population, can be prevented; but in order to prevent them the inhabitants of the world, and particularly those in overcrowded countries, must shoulder the responsibility for correcting existing evils rather than pass on to an ever-increasing posterity a fruitless struggle for existence against insuperable odds.

FIG. 99—A course for farmer coöperators conducted by the Famine Commission.

CHAPTER VIII

SOCIAL CURES FOR FAMINE

OVERPOPULATION MEANS POVERTY

There are some optimistic persons, scientists included, who do not view the rapid increase in the world's population with apprehension. The writer would suggest for such persons a few years' residence in interior China. Here one is brought face to face with the dire conditions that inevitably follow when the number of inhabitants is greater than the productivity of the land they occupy will support.

It may be suggested that productivity can be increased. This is certainly true. To quote again from Mr. H. B. Elliston of the Chinese Government Bureau of Economic Information:

Were scientific agriculture introduced on a wide scale, these lands could be made to yield more abundantly. But the country does not seem to have arrived at that stage yet, just as it is still in the dirt road stage of highway development. You cannot force material progress on a country. That comes from cooperation from within, which is again predicated on ability to absorb the fruits of such progress. You cannot persuade a farmer to buy an up-to-date plough if he is merely subsisting on the ragged edge of penury; if he is totally divorced from any help but that created by himself. It would therefore seem that age-old methods of agriculture will persist for many years to come.

Many foreigners are attacking the problem of helping China in the wrong way by not putting first emphasis on the increase of production. Humanitarian enterprises are legion in China, many of them supported solely by American funds. Their aim is to preserve the life of the people, to teach safeguards against disease and calamity. Thus, some of the erstwhile checks to over-population are in process of elimination; and coupled with the natural geometrical increase of the race, may in the course of time

179

outweigh other considerations in keeping China on the border line of economic endurance. The right way to help China is to intensify her productivity, so that it will be able to take care of the excessive population. Production should come before population in the humanitarian enterprises of the West, for population's sake. For what is the good of saving people from disease if finally they have to starve to death in the unequal striving for existence which is the constant battle of the majority of present-day Chinese?

But another question arises: Will the increase of production bring more comforts of life for the inhabitants, or will it simply result in an increasing number of people to share existing comforts?

It has already been stated that the population of China doubled between the middle of the eighteenth and the middle of the nineteenth century, and a steady increase has been made since that time. Europe has increased her population two and a half times in the last century. The world has doubled its numbers in sixty years. Japan's population of 56,000,000 in 1920 represents a doubling in forty years, but Japan has been rapidly industrialized. China's advance is below the average rate because the checks are more pronounced. But even at this reduced rate of increase there would be nearly 900,000,000 people in China in another century, or more than half of the present population of the world. The writer does not believe that this is going to happen, of course, but the *only factor to prevent it will be the failure of production to keep the pace*. What does this constant battle between production and population portend for China? It portends a century of abject poverty for the masses, the sort of poverty from which they are now suffering, but intensified. It can only be prevented if the fruits from improvements in agriculture, in trade, in distribution of population, and in the development of the country, are restricted to something like the present number of inhabitants. How is this going to be brought about when apparently the chief ambition of the Chinese is the rearing of offspring, when so much effort is now being spent to counteract the natural checks that heretofore have kept the population within bounds?

Education Needed

The cure for the social causes of famine is, in a word, education. This does not mean book learning alone but general enlightenment, particularly of the masses, and the rousing of public opinion. Up to the present time no scientific study has been made in China of important practical problems such as has been the rule in Western countries. Even supposing such studies had been made, dissemination of the results would be next to impossible on account of the low standard of education and the high percentage of illiteracy. Thus the subject must be treated from its very foundations. The literacy percentage must be increased while educators and social workers are doing more advanced research work.

The task is a herculean one, for the conditions which it is sought to improve are tending constantly to retard the work. Overcrowding renders the struggle for existence indescribably hard, and one can scarcely be blamed for finding it difficult to seek education on an empty stomach or after a day of strenuous labor. It has always been a marvel to the writer in view of these circumstances that there is such a love of learning among the people; but even with the willingness to undergo great hardships to gain knowledge, which is apparent on every side, there are surprisingly few who are able to get more than the most rudimentary education.

Mass Education Movement

One of the chief obstacles that confronts the educator is the difficulty of the language. There is no phonetic alphabet, the written language being represented by something like 25,000 different characters. Most of the texts, furthermore, contain so many characters, and the language has been so cumbered with allusions, making exact understanding difficult except for the really well educated, that the man of meager learning has been unable to make them out at all. This has led in recent years to a number of mass education movements. Various phonetic alphabets have been devised, but these do not meet the need, for China possesses a great number of quite dissimilar dialects. However, the written character always has the same meaning even though it is pronounced differently in the spoken languages of the country.

The most hopeful educational movement is one that is making very considerable progress at present. It is, briefly, an attempt to convey thought by the least possible number of written characters. Mr. Y. C. James Yen, the leader of the movement, is quoted in the China Year Book as having said:

> No greater contribution has ever been made to the cause of popular education in China than that made recently by the Literary Revolution in abolishing the classical language and adopting the pei-hua (spoken language) for all literary purposes. That the adoption of the pei-hua facilitates immensely the study of the Chinese language no one can dispute.

Mr. Yen then goes on to say that after several years of study by himself and his associates a course was developed consisting of a series of readers called "Foundation Characters," a course based on 1000 characters representing the words most commonly used in the spoken language. Mastery of this list will enable a man to write simple business letters, keep accounts, and read simple newspapers intelligently. It has been demonstrated that this can be accomplished by Chinese in four months by one and a half hours of daily study. The movement aims to reach the common people and is generally carried out by volunteer teachers or students who are recruited from the educated classes and who devote certain leisure hours to the work. In many cases the school buildings are used during hours when they are not required for the regular students. A demonstration of the effectiveness of this idea in a number of widely scattered cities led to the formation of an organization known as the National Popular Education Association, and extensive plans are being formulated to launch campaigns in all parts of the country. The greatest progress has, naturally, been made in the cities. The problem of reaching the country people is a much more difficult one.

This movement is described to show that there is now a growing tendency in China to undertake reforms. It is one of the signs that the present unsatisfactory situation is recognized and that the people mean to do something to remedy it. Such an enterprise together with kindred movements springing out of the literary renaissance should have the whole-hearted support of those who are desirous of seeing better times in China.

FIG. 100—A group of farmer coöperators, members of the China International Famine Relief Commission rural credit societies.

BIRTH CONTROL NEEDED

But while the spread of education and general enlightenment is a hopeful sign, it must be recognized that unless a conscious effort is made to lower the birth rate the effect of modern knowledge will do quite as much to increase population in China as to decrease it—probably more, in fact. The spread of modern ideas of sanitation, the proper control of contagious diseases, preventive medicine, and modern surgery will naturally greatly decrease the death rate—at least it should logically do so. It may mean, however, that the man who is saved from dying of cholera today will die of starvation tomorrow. Certainly this will happen if the death rate decreases materially and the birth rate remains at the same level, other factors remaining constant. The writer views this problem with such concern that he would even propose as a department of the work of every medical institution the teaching of methods of contraception. In this way the birth rate might be lowered at the same time with the death rate.

While it takes centuries to build up a population as large as that of China it would take a comparatively short time to reduce it to a size where the productivity of the land would support it in comfort. In fact, if the people should be content to have just half as many offspring during the next generation as were born during the last, the population would probably be so reduced that there would be plenty of food for all and no hardship whatever would be felt in the process. But birth control by the Chinese on any extensive scale is at present out of the question; years of strenuous work and a change in the basic social concepts of the Chinese must precede its realization.

There is nothing, so far as the writer can find, in the original Christian doctrine which cannot be reconciled to a scientific treatment of the question of eugenics of which a control of the birth rate, where it is excessively high, is an important factor. The objections which may be raised on religious grounds are, at least, much less fundamental with Christianity than they are with Confucianism. Thus the displacement of Confucianism in China by Christianity might conceivably make the work of the reformer less difficult. However, this is a hypothesis which cannot be proved for centuries to come, judging from the present registered rate of progress in the introduction of Christianity. It would appear in fact that a crusade must be carried on in China as elsewhere.

But even assuming that the psychology of the Chinese could be changed and that they could be induced to adopt preventive measures, the conditions under which most of them live are such that contraception could not be nearly so effective as in Western countries. The poverty of the people would prevent the purchase of drugs or the various preventive devices; also the tremendous task of teaching the people their use would be an obstacle of no mean proportions.

As was intimated in a previous chapter, the introduction of industrialism, if it produces the same reactions in China that it has abroad, will serve to check the birth rate; and the improvement in the standard of living resulting from it will act as a further retarding influence. It is possible also that the introduction of the Western form of life insurance and also more prosperous conditions will help to destroy the idea that it is necessary to rear many children in order to have sons to make provision for declining years.

The adoption and enforcement by the government of a marriage law establishing monogamy as the only recognized code might assist in a small way to decrease the number of births; and indeed government action along other lines connected with the population question would undoubtedly have effect.

THRIFT SOCIETIES

Education would also help to prevent much of the wastefulness of ceremonials. Of late years there has been a reaction against the old practices, and those Chinese who have had the advantage of foreign training are the most ardent in their effort to break the shackles imposed by custom. This tendency has asserted itself in the formation of "thrift societies," whose members bind themselves not to initiate or participate in feasts or other wasteful practices. The Y. M. C. A. has done much to develop this movement, and "thrift weeks" are now organized throughout the country, when a concentrated effort is made to reach as many people as possible with the message of the benefits of saving and the evil effects of wasteful ceremonies. This is accomplished through lectures, bulletins, and posters. The movement should be fostered and encouraged by all thinking people.

Education, again, must be relied upon to bring about the reform in foot binding. An unwittingly beneficial effect of the greed of a certain military official has come to the writer's notice. In one of the provinces where the custom of foot binding has been religiously followed even up to the present time, the military governor without any warning declared that it was to cease forthwith. However, it was provided that feet

could still be bound if a tax were paid. This tax was on a
sliding scale, all women over thirty being exempt. The rate
was highest for the youngest children, tapering off after the
marriageable age. It was provided that payments according

Fig. 101—The chief means of transportation in China. A small junk carries
very little sail.

to the age of the child concerned should be made at regular
intervals so long as her feet should be bound. This is certainly
a way to get results.

Influence of Western Civilization

Of late years with the development of transportation, the
improvement of communications, and the gradual opening
up of China, it has been borne in upon the people that a new
era has dawned, and their complacent self-sufficiency has
been rudely shocked. The impact of Western industrialism
has indeed shaken this great country to its foundations. It
has resulted in a transformation even of the form of government, it has served to develop a nationalistic spirit in some of
the people, it has set in motion forces that will eventually result in the complete emancipation of the Chinese women.
China is truly awakening although, because of the tremendous
field to be covered, progress is not rapid.

There has been a growing interest on the part of the Chinese in Western education for application to their own needs, an interest which has resulted in a marked increase in the number of natives who complete their education in

Fig. 102—Sailing over the inundated fields during the northern China floods of 1924.

foreign countries. There are several thousand Chinese students in the United States alone. Foreign schools in China (most of which are missionary institutions) have also met with much favor and have long waiting lists of applicants. The return to China of thousands of foreign university graduates has injected new life into the country. This group has founded the Chinese National Association for the Advancement of Education, which has undertaken the tremendous task of educational reform.

While progress has been made in the theory of modern organization, the practical side has also been mastered by a constantly growing number of foreign-trained mill operatives, mechanics, bank clerks, chauffeurs, and the like. It is quite generally conceded that the Chinese, under proper supervision, display as much ability in handling mechanical contrivances and in carrying out the routine clerical requirements of modern business as do Westerners. Thus, while there is a lack of inventive genius, it would appear that there is a capacity of imitation coupled with the ingenuity that has always been a characteristic of the race. We are justified in expecting an industrial expansion somewhat on the order of the development in Japan. The two principal factors working against the rapid industrialization of China, quite apart from lack of capital or credit organization, are the dishonesty of the officials, who prey on developments of all kinds, and the lack of coöperation on the part of the people. Remove these disabilities and there is no reason why China should not be the greatest industrial nation in the world. The country is rich in natural resources and has an unsurpassed abundance of cheap labor.

Chinese Fundamentally Sound

With the awakening of China will come more civic pride and more community spirit, and these things in turn will make for better living conditions. There are some confirmed pessimists about China who can see no future for her but a continuation of the present chaos and ultimate breakdown and disintegration; but, although there may be great political changes and realignments, there are still four hundred million Chinese people; and, if history teaches us anything, she teaches that a race as numerous and as fundamentally sound as the Chinese, which has maintained its political and cultural solidarity for so many centuries, will not perish from the earth.

Fig. 103—Sunrise over the sacred Hwa Shan.   (Photograph by C. W. Bishop.)

CONCLUSIONS

The chronic famine situation in China cannot be adequately relieved without a stable and effective government. This does not mean, however, that no amelioration can be achieved during these disordered times. Any doubt on that score has been removed by the operations during the past six years of the China International Famine Relief Commission and its constituent committees.

There are some lines of work that will yield results more quickly than others. In order of importance they are:

1. Flood control, irrigation, land reclamation.
2. Economic improvement, rural credits, colonization, home and village industry.
3. Improved agriculture and forestation.
4. Development of transportation.
5. Education.

Several of these might be undertaken at once. In fact all of them should be pressed as vigorously as possible, and it should be noted that some progress is actually being made day by day in several of these directions. But on account of the limited funds at the disposal of coöperative enterprise, the undertakings that would be most quickly productive should be put in the forefront.

Many persons will not agree with the writer as to this arrangement. For instance, some will doubt the wisdom of putting education last when the reduction of the birth rate is so vital to the prosperity of the people of China and hence to the famine problem of the future. But even the most sanguine will agree that modification of the fundamental concepts of the people will be a very slow and expensive process. What is needed is the immediate release of the masses from the constant threat of starvation. This will in itself create conditions where education can be appreciated and where more thought can be devoted to the larger social aspects of life.

The greatest immediate benefit to the nation will come from insurance of the crops against flood and drought and provision of means to increase the area of cultivable land and the yield on the fields already worked. This can be done by flood control, irrigation, land reclamation, and other similar projects which modern engineering has made possible. The cost of such work in China, where human labor is plentiful and cheap, is relatively small compared with the benefits which result; and the effect is at once apparent, even minor projects bringing prosperity almost immediately to thousands of people. Although the largest schemes must wait for better political conditions, there are almost unlimited fields for work on problems of small dimensions.

Next to conservancy, the most quickly productive work is the economic improvement of the rural population by the provision of better credit facilities, by the introduction of home and village industries, by colonization, and similar enterprises. Most of these, except colonization, can be undertaken at once and carried forward even under present conditions in China. Improved agriculture and forestation might also be included in this category; but they are more difficult to bring about, and their benefits are not so quickly apparent.

The development of transportation is important, but in its effects on the famine problem it is put fourth. There are already existing trunk lines which serve the provinces that are most susceptible to distress, and the cost of extending the system is at present almost prohibitive. Quicker results can be effected by using funds for conservancy or rural improvement.

Education, in its broader sense, is the fundamental cure for the ills not only of China but of the world. It goes hand in hand with the projects of improvement listed above—

in fact, it may even be considered an integral part of every one of them. Education is used here not in its broad sense but in the commonly accepted meaning of the acquisition of knowledge from books, and hence is put at the end of the list.

And now for a final word about the population problem. In the writer's opinion it is overpopulation that constitutes the fundamental reason for the recent famines in China. Futhermore, overpopulation is now a matter of world concern. What has occurred in China, will if the human race lets nature take her course, most certainly occur in other lands which are now prosperous. If a pair of rabbits are shut in an enclosure which has a limited area of good grass they will be comfortably provided for; but their numerous progeny will have very hard scratching unless some altruistic person throws in fodder from outside. There are optimists among us who ascribe to Providence this rôle of benefactor to the ever increasing human race, but they fail to take cognizance of the fact that no bountiful showers of manna have fallen in China. And who will say that there is no need?

INDEX

Adoption, 91

Agriculture, 38; antiquated methods, 24; intensive, 25, 27; scientific, 109, 179; teaching, 4

American Red Cross, 32, 49; China Famine Relief, 172; Hwai River conservancy, 152; road construction plan, 174; wells for irrigation, 148–149

Ancestor worship, 88, 90, 100; effect on birth rate, 88

Ancestral tablets, 90

Anhwei, 45, 48, 49

Animals, domestic, 78; improvement, 114

Arable land, 118

Armies, 20; army on the march, 64 (ill.); cost, 78; disbandment, 164; excess troops, 77

Artisans, 128

Authority, 67

Baker, J. E., 33, 35

Banditry, 75, 119, 123; Shensi refuge from bandits, 77 (ill.)

Banking, 3, 21; rural, 129

Bard, Émile, 70

Bean cake and oil, 112

Bean flour, 113

Beans, 112

Beggars, 1, 11 (ill.)

Berczeller, L., 113

Binding the feet, 98, 185

Birth control, 183, 191

Birth rate, 4, 17, 87, 189, 190; ancestor worship as related to, 88; concubinage and, 91

Birthday celebrations, 93–94

Bishop, C. W., 82, 189

Boats, families living in, at flood times, 117 (ill.); sailing over inundated fields in 1924, 187 (ill.); Yangtze junks and steamers, 133 (ill.)

Borrowers, 22

Boxer Rebellion, 66

Buddhists, 100

Budgets, family, 7

Burgess, J. S., 11

Burial, 98, 100

Business soundness, 170

Buxton, L. H. D., 45, 119

Canals, 34; irrigation, 144, 145, 148

Cannibalism, 40

Canton, 171; dike improvement scheme, 72

Canton Christian College, 114

Capture of citizens, 76

Carriers, human, 32, 33 (ill.)

Carts, 139; flooded roads and, 135 (ill.); with the narrow tires, 31 (ill.)

Cave dwellings, loess, 61 (ill.)

Caves, 62

Census, 84, 85

Ceremonials, waste, 93, 185

Chairs for travel, 103 (ill.)

Chang-chao-lan, 68

Charity, 106, 172

Chekiang, 15, 40, 41, 42, 45; fields destroyed, 58

Chen, Ta, 12, 120

Chenfu, 12

Chengtu plain, irrigation, 142, 144

Ch'ien Lung, 85, 108

Chihli, 10, 15, 29, 40, 41, 45; dike break, 55 (ill.); flood around Hsin-An, 36 (ill.); flood of 1924, 53, 56; flood preventon plain, 160; ice in flooded area, 89 (ill.); river systems and flood areas, 52, 159 (map)

Children, 88, 90; adoption, 91; sale, 2

China, 1; lowlands and river basins, 6 (map); population increase and area, 108; self-support, 108–109

China Continuation Committee, 16; census, 85–86